WE FLOURISH

A GUIDE TO SUPPORTING PROACTIVE MENTAL HEALTH AT WORK

JUDD ALLEN, Ph.D.

Human Resources Institute, LLC
www.healthyculture.com
151 Dunder Road
Burlington, Vermont 05401 USA
JuddA@healthyculture.com
(802) 862-8855

Ordering Information
Quantity sales. Special discounts are available on quantity purchases by organizations, associations, and others. For details, contact the publisher.
Library of Congress Cataloging-in-Publication Data
Names: Allen, Judd, 1958-author.
We Flourish: A Guide for Supporting Proactive Mental Health at Work
Description: Burlington, Vermont: HealthyCulture.com [2022] ⊢ Includes bibliographical references.
Identifiers: eBook ISBN 978-0-941703-46-8; paperback ISBN 978-0-941703-44-4
Subjects: NONFICTION/ Motivational Management & Leadership/
Workplace Culture/Human Resources & Personnel Management

Cover photograph of Judd Allen by Karen Pike of www.kpikephoto.com.

Contents

Acknowledgments

MY FATHER, ROBERT ALLEN, PH.D., inspired my interest in supportive cultural environments. This book is a tribute to his life's work.

I would like to thank my colleagues, Don Ardell, Michael Arloski, David Ballard, William Baun, Craig Becker, Jim Carmen, Dee Edington, Bill Hettler, Tad Mitchell, Michael O'Donnell, Gillian Pieper, Kay Ryan, Richard Safeer, Samia Simurro, Marie-Josee Shaar, Ewa Stelmasiak, Elaine Sullivan, and Jack Travis. These leaders share a vision that includes both kindness and flourishing.

My close friends and family generously provided their feedback. Mollie Allen, Richard Blount, Jonathan Sands, Tere Gade, and Mary Sochet were a big help.

We Flourish benefited from thoughtful editing by Candi Cross and Tere Gade.

Statement about Inclusive Language

This is a book about mental health and emotional well-being. We now know that humans are extraordinarily diverse in sexual identity and sexual orientation. The English language needs to honor that diversity. In this book, I'm choosing language that is intended to honor that diversity. So, where you may have seen *he/she*, I'm going to use *they* or *them*.

Chapter 1

To Flourish: An Introduction

To flourish
1: to grow luxuriantly: THRIVE
2a: to achieve success: PROSPER
b: to be in a state of activity or production
c: to reach a height of development or influence

—"FLOURISH." MERRIAM-WEBSTER.COM
DICTIONARY, MERRIAM-WEBSTER

THERE IS A riveting, inspiring story to be written about how your employees joined with organizational leaders to dramatically reduce mental illness and to increase overall mental well-being. This page turner is a story about both enhancing individual resilience and about creating a mentally healthy work environment. The story is about changing the organizational culture to support proactive mental health behaviors and attitudes.

Flourishing is a team sport. We do this together. From large mammals, bats and shrimp to fish, coral and ants, the animal planet is a quintessential role model for thriving together to get ahead in hunting and gathering, protecting each other, and traveling hundreds of miles for the right environment to rest, replenish resources, and restore. Humans seem particularly well-equipped for flourishing. We possess multiple magnificent types of intelligence that can advance our species, generation to generation.

Flourishing Our Way Out of the Mental Illness Crisis

So, how are we humans presently doing with the goal of flourishing? At present, flourishing seems out of reach. Our current mental illness crisis tends to overwhelm our dreams for flourishing. In the United States, almost half of adults (46.4 percent) will experience a mental illness during their lifetimes. Every year, more than 12 billion working days are lost due to mental illness. Between 2010 and 2030, mental illness will cost the global economy $16 USD trillion in lost economic output—more than cancer, diabetes, and respiratory diseases combined. Your organization and team cannot afford the upended lives, lost productivity, and increased health care costs.

Maybe you and your employees will be among the lucky ones to experience lifelong mental health. You may not experience mental illness, but don't count on it. Twenty-one percent of U.S. adults experienced mental illness in 2020 (52.9 million people). This represents one in five adults.

The pandemic of COVID-19 revealed the inadequacy

of our current approach to mental health, which focuses almost exclusively on treatment and not on prevention. Our system was overwhelmed prior to new pandemic stressors. Here is a snapshot of those stressors from a report of findings from a survey issued by American Psychological Association (APA) in October 2020. It is highly likely that your employees are experiencing many, if not most, of these mental and physical health challenges.

- **A majority of adults (61%) reported experiencing undesired weight changes since the start of the pandemic,** with more than 2 in 5 (42%) saying they gained more weight than they intended. Of this group, adults reported gaining an average of 29 pounds (with a typical gain of 15 pounds, which is the median).

- **Two in 3 Americans (67%) said they are sleeping more or less than they wanted to since the pandemic started.** Similar proportions reported less (35%) and more (31%) sleep than desired. Nearly 1 in 4 adults (23%) reported drinking more alcohol to cope with their stress during the coronavirus pandemic.

- **Nearly half of Americans (47%) said they delayed or canceled health care services** since the pandemic started.

- **Nearly half of parents (48%) said the level of stress in their life has increased compared with before the pandemic.** More than 3 in 5 parents with children who are still home for remote learning (62%) said the same.

- **Essential workers were more than twice as likely as those who are not to have received treatment from** a mental health professional (34% vs. 12%) and to have been diagnosed with a mental health disorder since the coronavirus pandemic started (25% vs. 9%).

- **Black Americans were most likely to report feelings of concern about the future.** More than half said they feel uneasy about adjusting to in-person interaction once the pandemic ends (57% vs. 51% Asian, 50% Hispanic and 47% white).

- **Gen Z adults (46%) were the most likely generation to say that their mental health has worsened** compared with before the pandemic, followed by Xers (33%), Millennials (31%), Boomers (28%) and older adults (9%).

Simply put, mental health professionals cannot treat all those afflicted with anxiety, depression, alcoholism, substance abuse, bipolar affective disorder, dissociation, dissociative disorders, eating disorders, obsessive compulsive disorder, paranoia, post-traumatic stress disorder, psychosis, and schizophrenia. For too many of us, mental health treatment is out of reach.

The current approach is costing a fortune in economic and human terms. However, it only addresses the needs of those currently afflicted with mental illness. Ideally, we would be both treating mental illness and increasing mental well-being. Little is being done to prevent mental illness. And less is being done to promote great mental health by living productive, happy, and healthy lives.

Health encapsulates more than just not being sick.

Health addresses the needs of the whole person. The goal is to achieve optimal quality of life. Proactive mental health embraces strategies that make us more resilient and help us to quickly recover from mental illness.

Shifting the culture towards proactive mental health begins with an agreement that our current approach, which focused almost exclusively on treating mental illness through therapy and drugs, cannot address the conditions needed to be resilient and thrive. When it comes to worker mental health, treatment is the right thing to do and important, but prevention is the preferred approach for electrifying a state of flourishing—and ultimately, flourishing together as a team.

Your organization and team cannot afford the lost productivity and increased health care. We need to proactively support mental health by adopting practices that lower the risks and speed recovery from mental illness. Helping your employees to achieve strong mental health is a paramount business strategy.

Shattering Cultural Myths about Mental Illness and Health

We Flourish challenges several widely held cultural beliefs about mental health and wellness. Debunking the following myths jump-starts our journey toward proactive mental health.

Cultural myth: Few people experience mental illness.

Fact: Roughly 21 percent of people are currently experiencing mental illness, and nearly 50% of people will experience such challenges over the course of their lifetimes.

Cultural myth: The current mental illness treatment options of therapy and medications are available and affordable.

Fact: There are long wait lists for mental illness treatment. It is expensive. We need alternatives including strategies that prevent mental illness. Proactive mental health can help address these challenges.

Cultural myth: Little can be done to prevent mental illness.

Fact: Health behaviors such as regular exercise, social engagement, employment, and relaxation techniques can help prevent mental illness.

Cultural myth: Mental health is merely the absence of mental illness.

Fact: Mental health is a quality-of-life concept directed at optimal emotional and mental well-being. Health is not just about avoiding illness. It includes enjoying optimal well-being. It is also true that some people can have a mental illness and still enjoy other aspects of their lives where they are experiencing high mental well-being.

Cultural myth: Mental illness is exclusively an individual problem.

Fact: Unsupportive cultural environments play a major role in undermining peoples' mental health. An example is how stressors at work and at home can disrupt healthy sleep. In addition, current cultural norms make seeking mental health treatment uncomfortable. We need to create cultural environments that support healthy behavior and make it more likely people will get the help needed to address mental illness.

Fortunately, you can co-create proactive mental health cultures that dramatically reduce the likelihood of mental illness while improving overall well-being and productivity. *We Flourish* explains how you can align cultural norms, shared values, peer support, workplace policies, and the overall social climate with proactive mental health. Your team will enjoy a proactive mental health culture that fully embraces:

- **Safety**—economic, physical, and emotional security
- **Connection**—positive and empowering relationships among coworkers, immediate supervisor/managers, housemates, family, and friends
- **Purpose**—meaning at work and outside of work
- **Presence**—mindfulness, inner peace, and an enjoyment of the here and now
- **Health Behavior**—preventive medicine, physical activity, and healthy eating
- **Adaptability**—personal growth, goal achievement and affirmative responses to change

The goal of *We Flourish* is to empower you to co-create the proactive mental health culture you and your co-workers want and need. Each *We Flourish* chapter defines key concepts, provides measurement tools, and highlights opportunities for constructive change. In Chapter 2, take a self-assessment of proactive mental health. Learn how my personal biography raised my awareness about mental health. Read case examples of employee experiences. In Chapter 3, learn about culture building blocks. In Chapter 4, learn how to increase the quantity and quality of peer support for personal change. Coworkers, immediate supervisors, family, and friends can assist their peers in achieving lasting lifestyle changes. In Chapter 5, develop your skills for fostering a supportive social climate. You'll learn to how assess the climate and offer strategies for strengthening the sense of community, shared vision, and positive outlook. In Chapter 6, examine cultural norms and how to align fourteen day-to-day norm influences (such as rewards, traditions, and training) with proactive mental health. In Chapter 7, learn about 26 workplace strategies that support employees' sense of personal purpose. In Chapter 8, develop a culture change plan. Adopt a step-by-step approach that will build and sustain a workplace that fully supports proactive mental health.

The positive approach to proactive mental health is a departure from long-established ways many of us view work. Historically, work was seen as a necessary compromise between financial necessity and personal well-being. In the broader culture, it was the norm to dread Mondays and to celebrate Fridays (TGIF). Retirement is a popular professional goal. According to this cultural perspective, our happy days would be spent *away* from work.

There have been many ways work and workplaces have undermined mental health. Unsafe working conditions, abusive leaders, low wages, and excessive work demands are all too common. However, there is a better way. We can break the traditional patterns and establish supportive cultural environments that embrace both individual well-being and successful organizations.

Make Proactive Mental Health Personal

"Sometimes self-care is exercise and eating right. Sometimes it's spending time with loved ones or taking a nap... Whatever soothes your soul."

—NANEA HOFFMAN

AT THE INDIVIDUAL level, proactive mental health is an overlapping matrix of six building blocks of behaviors and attitudes that prevent mental illness and increase overall mental well-being.

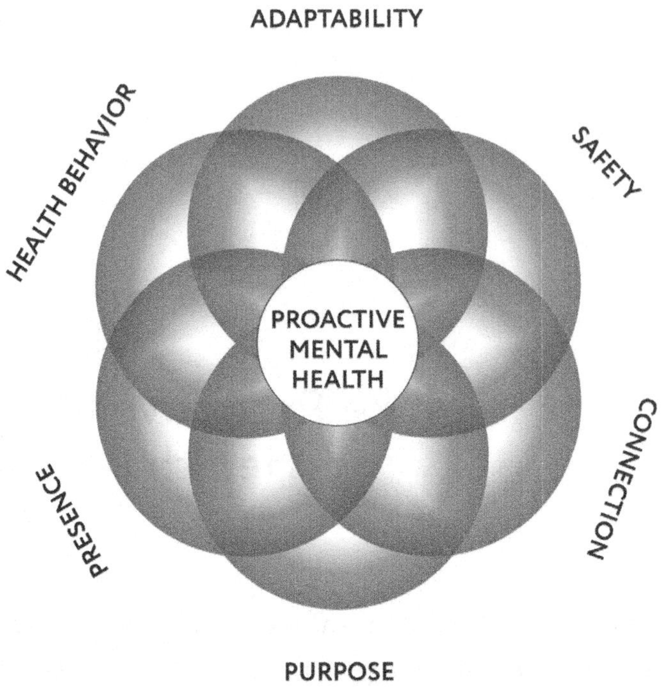

ADAPTABILITY

HEALTH BEHAVIOR

SAFETY

PROACTIVE
MENTAL
HEALTH

PRESENCE

CONNECTION

PURPOSE

Figure 1. Proactive Mental Health Matrix

- **Safety**—economic, physical, and emotional security
- **Connection**—positive and empowering relationships among coworkers, immediate supervisor/managers, housemates, family, and friends
- **Purpose**—meaning at work and outside of work
- **Presence**—mindfulness, inner peace, and an enjoyment of the here and now
- **Health Behavior**—preventive medicine, physical activity, and healthy eating
- **Adaptability**—personal growth, goal achievement and affirmative responses to change

When helping others, self-analysis and reflection are often good places to start. How are you? How do you feel? How is your proactive mental health? The following confidential self-assessment offers a snapshot of your personal proactive mental health.

Proactive Mental Health Self-Assessment

Proactive mental health is a constellation of 26 behaviors and attitudes that reduce the likelihood of mental illness and increase overall mental well-being. The following confidential proactive mental health self-assessment asks about your current practices and about the importance of each practice to your mental health. Your answers will help prioritize efforts to support mental health.

Instructions: *Using the five-point scale, rate how consistently you experience the proactive mental health attitudes and behaviors.*

5 Always
4 Often
3 Sometimes
2 Rarely
1 Never
NA Not applicable

How are you doing this week?

ATTITUDES AND BEHAVIORS	Current Practice
Presence	
Are you able to focus on the here-and-now?	5 4 3 2 1 NA
Do you declutter and destress your life so you can experience inner peace?	5 4 3 2 1 NA
Do you practice daily stress management techniques such as taking a walk, meditation, or yoga?	5 4 3 2 1 NA
Connection	
Are you able to love and be loved?	5 4 3 2 1 NA
Do you spend time with friends most days?	5 4 3 2 1 NA
Can you forgive?	5 4 3 2 1 NA
Are you grateful?	5 4 3 2 1 NA
Can you trust others, and are you trustworthy?	5 4 3 2 1 NA
Are you good at teamwork?	5 4 3 2 1 NA
Adaptability	
Can you handle disappointment?	5 4 3 2 1 NA
Do you persist in the face of challenges?	5 4 3 2 1 NA
Are you open to trying new ways of doing things?	5 4 3 2 1 NA
Do you consider your strengths before taking on tasks and challenges?	5 4 3 2 1 NA
Do you avoid seeing problems or bad news as permanent, pervasive (affecting all things), or personal (about you)?	5 4 3 2 1 NA

ATTITUDES AND BEHAVIORS	Current Practice
Purpose	
Do you feel like you are making a difference?	5 4 3 2 1 NA
Do you regularly do things that give your life meaning?	5 4 3 2 1 NA
Do you experience passion and commitment?	5 4 3 2 1 NA
Safety	
Do you feel economically secure?	5 4 3 2 1 NA
Are you free from physical and emotional violence and abuse?	5 4 3 2 1 NA
Do you live, work, and play in healthy physical environments?	5 4 3 2 1 NA
Health Behavior	
Are you current on your preventive medical health screenings?	5 4 3 2 1 NA
Do you get help with mental and physical health problems early on?	5 4 3 2 1 NA
Do you eat a healthy diet?	5 4 3 2 1 NA
Are you free from addictions to alcohol and other drugs?	5 4 3 2 1 NA
Do you get adequate rest?	5 4 3 2 1 NA

Review your responses. How are you doing with your proactive mental health? You can be mentally healthy without achieving all 26 practices. Most people completing this self-assessment identify both personal strengths and opportunities for improvement. Physical activity, healthy eating, adequate sleep, and improved social relationships are among the most common goals. Many people are also helping a coworker, friend, or family member to achieve their proactive mental health goals. This high level of interest in achieving proactive mental health and in helping others with their mental well-being provides a solid foundation for initiating personal and organizational change. People usually don't need to be convinced of the importance of these goals; instead, we can turn our attention to supporting people in achieving their personal goals.

My Proactive Mental Health Story

Cultural support, mental health and mental illness have been important topics in my life. Like me, many members of my immediate family are psychologists, social workers, and psychiatrists. My father, Robert Allen, Ph.D. attributed our family's passion for mental health to a lesson learned from his father (my grandfather), Ed Allen. Ed was wounded in World War I. During his hospitalization, he became addicted to morphine. He was able to overcome his addiction but was unable to shake the war trauma he experienced. He spent his adult life in and out of mental health services, unable to work, and lived from disability checks. He was ashamed about his inability to hold a job. Fortunately, his spirits lifted when he reached retirement age. He redefined himself as *retired*. This new retired status allowed him to face the world without shame. The culture did not support people with mental illnesses, like my grandfather. However, the culture was supportive of retired men. In my grandfather's story, we saw the meaningful interaction between culture and mental illness. Like my father (also a psychologist), I have dedicated my life's work to creating supportive cultural environments for mental health.

We Flourish is the culmination of more than sixty years of helping groups and organizations build caring communities. My father formed our company, the Human Resources Institute (HRI), in the 1960s. His first book, *Collegefields: From Delinquency to Freedom*, centers on creating supportive cultural environments that overcome juvenile delinquency. His other books, *The Quiet Revolution, Beat the System, Lifegain,* and *The Organizational Unconscious*, are about creating kind and productive organizational cultures.

Since my father's death in 1987, I have authored more than fifty books, book chapters, movies, and journal articles on culture change. HRI has assisted more than a thousand businesses, health care institutions, universities, government agencies and community organizations to create healthier and more productive cultural environments. The skills and knowledge we have developed provide insight into ways to improve the current mental health crisis gripping our nation. *We Flourish* explains how you can envision and co-create cultures that no longer engender mental illness but create social environments supporting proactive mental health.

The wellness and health promotion movements provide a foundation for key ideas in *We Flourish*. HRI assisted in the development of many of the early corporate wellness programs during the 1970s. Over the past fifty years, employers have been offering programs and services designed to support healthier lifestyles. The original wellness vision focused on both quality of life and the whole person. However, in practice, worksite health promotion focused on avoiding health risks rather than on thriving. The promotion of physical activity, healthy eating, smoking cessation, and health screenings did not fully take mental health into consideration.

We Flourish was written to help address the limitations on the current worksite wellness program model. We will be offering strategies to address the mental wellness goals currently underdeveloped in worksite wellness programs.

Gaining Proactive Mental Health Perspective

Unless you are new to your organization, you have been acculturated. Your attitudes and understandings related to mental health and illness have been shaped by your culture. For instance, in many workplaces, the strong norm is to avoid discussing mental health until someone is in crisis. We sweep such discussions under the rug until they unavoidably interfere with work. The corollary norm likely in your work environment is to think of mental health and illness as primarily a concern for individual employees rather than something to be addressed at the team or organization levels. Also extremely likely, goals for creating a supportive proactive mental health culture have not yet been a part of the conversation.

Your efforts to lead change would benefit from an independent perspective, making it easier to see what is possible. You would benefit from knowing how similar organizations under similar circumstances were successful in supporting their employees' mental health. Ideally, you would make decisions based on a large list of "best practice" organizations.

My consulting work made it possible to see workplaces address proactive mental health and overall well-being. The perspective provided by working with multiple worksites has made it easier for me to identify opportunities for change. Over the years, I've invited my graduate students to read case studies describing workplaces and jobs. My assignment asked them to think about the work environments described in the studies and then write an essay about how the culture would change to better support health and well-being. My favorite books for these assignments are:

- *The 100 Best Companies to Work for in America* (3rd Revised Ed.), by Robert Levering and Milton Moskowitz

- *Working: People Talk About What They Do All Day and How They Feel About What They Do*, by Studs Terkel

- *Gig: Americans Talk About Their Jobs*, edited by John Bowe, Marisa Bowe, Sabin Streeter with Darron Murphy, and Rose Kernochan

Both *Working* and *Gig* are written from the employees' perspectives. They describe how it is to work in dozens of different jobs, ranging from a prostitute to a high school basketball coach. The *100 Best Companies* feature descriptions of companies ranked as outstanding places to work.

The following fictional case stories highlight the goals of proactive mental health in a variety of work environments. Like my graduate students, practice your skills by applying them to common and somewhat familiar work settings. The stories are of a nurse, a teacher, and a young man working in fast food restaurant, a human resource director, and a factory worker. Almost all of us have had some exposure to these jobs either through personal experience or through the news media. Use your imagination to fill in some of the stories' gaps.

- What are the cultural strengths and what opportunities for improvement exist within each work environment?

- How could we address each of the six dimensions of proactive mental health?

- If you were a consultant to this organization, what would be your recommendations?

Kay Hopkins, Oncology Nurse

Nurse Kay Hopkins worked in the oncology unit of a regional medical center. She loved her work even though many of her patients were struggling with terminal illnesses. According to Kay, "The most rewarding part of my job is helping patients and their families navigate difficult conversations and decisions and helping them to feel safe through what is usually a very scary time." She chose to go into nursing 10 years ago after caring for several close family members through terminal illnesses. She held the nurses they encountered in high regard, and hoped that a nursing career would be rewarding, and give her the financial means to support herself and her daughter.

Safety

Kay knew she had job security. The nursing shortage virtually assured her of full employment for as long as she wanted. The pay, which had been inadequate early in her career, was sufficient to keep her little family solvent.

She felt physically safe most of the time. The late-night walk to the parking garage made her anxious. Now, seniority meant better daytime shifts.

Emotional security was still an issue. Some oncology doctors behaved like prima donnas. Several had short tempers and were not exactly respectful to woman nurses. Kay knew firsthand that any complaint was going nowhere. These docs were cash cows for the medical center.

Presence

The oncology unit was perpetually short-staffed. Everything was "stat." There was no time for reflection or even to eat a meal. It took Kay an hour after work to get her head together and relax.

Connections

Irregular work shifts interfered with Kay's ability to make friends at work and outside of work. Kay often did not know which shift she would be working until the last minute. If someone called in sick, she might be asked to fill in. Such requests, although never welcome, pulled at her heart strings. Kay knew what it was like when they were short-handed.

Kay loved spending time supporting her patients and their families. In better times she used to feel like she had become a member of her patients' families. The nursing shortage and slim staffing in general deprived Kay of what she liked best about nursing. There was no longer time for being any more than professional and friendly.

Adaptability

There was a time when the positive social atmosphere at work was uplifting. New approaches to cancer treatment and innovations in patient care were readily embraced. Kay embraced being a role model for her patients and their families. For example, Kay adopted a new diet to reduce cancer risks. She wanted to practice what she preached. Those days were gone. Health professionals were now just trying to survive the increased workload. Anything new was looked at with outright derision.

Kay didn't know who she would turn to with a work-related suggestion or concern. Kay knew no one in administration now. With ever changing staffing, Kay did not even feel she was part of a team.

Health Behavior

Like most of her colleagues, Kay had put on some weight. Irregular shifts made it difficult to maintain a regular exercise routine. Her lack of fitness felt especially wrong. Kay knew better.

Fortunately, Kay was current on her health screenings and unlike several of her peers, was able to steer clear of heavy drinking. Kay knew that several of her colleagues were taking advantage of easy access to prescriptions and the pharmacy. She hoped to avoid using drugs to sleep better after stressful shifts.

Purpose

Nursing always gave Kay a strong sense of personal purpose. She loved helping patients and their families. Patient education was her forte. She often felt as if she had become a member of her patients' families. However, the lack of staffing cut into opportunities to sit and talk with patients and their families. Kay could not remember the last time she was able to stand still or sit. This constraint cut Kay off from the meaning she once gained from nursing.

Finally, a bad Friday ensued in her tenth year of nursing. That day, Kay wrestled with Dietary to provide an extra salad for a patient, she had a battle with Laundry to retrieve some sheets, and it took her three hours to get Housekeeping to help her clean up a mess of broken dishes when a patient tipped over his bed tray. She had just worked a double shift and realized that in a few weeks, she'd be going day to night duty again. She wondered where to turn with her complaints, but all around her were others with problems no more difficult than here. Exhausted and frustrated, thinking of her three-year-old at the day-care center, she quit.

Jack Burak, High School Math and Computer Science Teacher

In the high school, Jack Burak is known as Mr. Burak. He's been teaching math and computer science for six years. Unlike many of the other teachers, he keeps his classes under control. Everyone sits at their desks relatively quiet and cooperative. Early on, he realized his students were capable of only "the very basic stuff." For example, he avoids covering word problems in algebra because his kids "want to do the absolute minimum." He lowered his expectation and made everything a lot easier. He is concerned, however, that his students lack preparation for college or for a job that requires math.

Safety

Student fights happen daily, and some students have been apprehended with guns. Although one of his job responsibilities, Mr. Burak hesitates before breaking up fights.

This year, there was a four-hour lockdown while the police searched for an intruder. During the lockdown, panic spread among students, faculty, and staff.

Mr. Burak feels secure in his job. The other teachers are "getting away with showing videos during class time while they read the newspaper." By his own reckoning, his professionalism is a notch above his colleagues.

Mr. Burak's pay hasn't kept up with inflation, but his medical benefits and retirement package seem satisfactory. He feels lucky that he doesn't have a family to support.

Presence

There are few breaks during the school day. He doesn't go to the teacher's lounge because the conversation always devolves to griping about the individual students and the school. There is no other place to relax and reflect. Sometimes he sits and eats lunch in his car.

Connections

Mr. Burak has not made friends at the school as one of the few male teachers. He often feels lonely and sometimes fantasizes about having an affair with a coworker. He does his job and goes home.

Adaptability

Mr. Burak found it easy to adapt to remote learning during the pandemic. He was quick to set up Zoom classes. He did not mind staying at home. However, he is glad to be teaching in a classroom again.

Health Behavior

Mr. Burak manages a variety of health risks. The food in the cafeteria is greasy, salty, and generally inedible. Some teachers bring baked goods to share in the teacher's lounge. Mr. Burak is putting on extra pounds. His apathy seems to have spread to other parts of his life. He has little interest in staying fit or eating well. There is no time to exercise during the school day. He wished he could take a nap, as insomnia has become a problem.

Mr. Burak tries to catch up on his fitness goals during

school breaks and long summer vacations. Last summer, he took several bike rides and even hiked up a nearby mountain. When school started, he fell back into his prior level of lethargy.

Purpose

Mr. Burak is still excited about the future of computer science. During the pandemic, his familiarity with computers has made him more valuable to the school, his co-workers, and students.

When he finished college, Mr. Burak was sure he could make a difference in the lives of his future students. He's given up on his ability to teach. He recognizes the apathy is widespread. By example, less than five percent of parents come to parent-teacher conferences. The joy and purpose have gone out of teaching. He's just putting in his time until retirement…many years away.

Alex Hoover, Fast Food Restaurant Employee

Alex is a sixteen-year-old sophomore in high school who works at a fast-food restaurant. The restaurant is located at a busy intersection and has a takeout window. He started working soon after his birthday to help support his family and to earn some extra spending money. His weekday shifts start at 6:00 and go until 9:00. He often covers weekend shifts. Alex rotates between the job of taking orders and the job of preparing and bagging foods.

Safety

Alex is gay. His immediate supervisor openly shares his religious belief that homosexuality is a sin. His co-workers ridicule gay customers and often direct their barbs at Alex. Alex is looking forward to being in places more accepting of his sexual orientation.

Fast food restaurants are commonly robbed, particularly at night. While Alex has yet to witness such an incident, he has heard stories. There are cameras in the ceiling, but Alex has noticed they are pointed at workspaces. The managers distrust those working the register.

Alex is concerned about being laid off. He is pretty sure that if the labor market was not so tight, he would be shown the door. Prominent signs inform customers there are jobs available with a starting salary higher than Alex's.

Presence

Alex barely has time to think. A timer starts when an order is taken and tracks when the order is served. The entire process is highly efficient but requires constant attention to details. There are short breaks, not long enough to leave the restaurant. During his breaks, Alex tries to find a quiet table to do his homework.

Connections

Alex has made one friend who is nervous about being identified as gay. The rest of the staff seem to have fun together. Alex feels like an outsider. Between schoolwork and the restaurant, Alex does not have time to get together with friends. He barely sees his family who also work long hours.

Adaptability

Alex is trying to adjust to his working conditions, but it is hard. The work is highly repetitive. Although there was talk of advancement and college benefits, Alex doesn't think they will apply to him.

Health Behavior

Those working at the restaurant receive a steep discount. Unfortunately, the menu lacks healthy choices. Alex selects the salad and tries to pick out the croutons. He drinks water although only served in bottles. He hates paying for water.

His busy school and work schedule cuts into exercise time. Alex loves to run and dance. Whenever he gets the chance, he takes a jog. The restaurant is sponsoring a local fun run and is even supplying t-shirts to employees. Alex is hoping the manager will give him the day off so he can join the fun run.

Purpose

Alex is glad he can earn some money while in high school. His parents are grateful, as money is tight. He doesn't see much of a future in fast food. He also knows the food is not healthy for the customers.

Brenda Johnson, Director of Human Resources

Brenda began her career as a social worker at a state agency helping people return to work after an illness or injury. Social work was particularly gratifying to Brenda, as she was a good listener and very resourceful at lining up support services. However, the pay was inadequate to cover basic household expenses and put her kids through college. She jumped at the opportunity to take a human resources director job at a manufacturing plant and is approaching her one-year work anniversary.

Safety

While her social work job was secure, the new HR position is less reliable. The biggest threat is a likely change at the top. The CEO is approaching retirement and there is some likelihood the company will change ownership. Sometimes new leaders bring in their own team of executive leadership.

Brenda's much higher salary allows her to cover college tuition for her kids and even take a mid-winter vacation to Florida.

Brenda is the only woman on the executive team not used to sharing decisions with women executives. For them, human resources is a soft area of business requiring a woman's sensitivities. Brenda feels like she must show she is as hardnosed as the men; however, tough talk and the rough treatment of employees make her uncomfortable.

Presence

Brenda has her own office and controls her own work schedule with an assistant to manage many day-to-day tasks. She schedules a full lunch hour most days, during which she does a fifteen-minute meditation.

Connections

Brenda does not have close friends at work. While people are friendly, she wishes she had one good friend to confide in. The hierarchy in her company and her male peers at the executive level don't feel like friendship material.

Adaptability

Brenda is comfortable adapting to changing circumstances. When COVID-19 hit, she sprang into action by developing new work from home policies. She addressed the temporary layoffs and got people back on board when work at the plant recommenced.

Brenda is excited about growing her human resources skills. She belongs to the local chapter of the Society for Human Resource Management, attending their meetings and some HR seminars online. The last seminar was on appreciative inquiry. She looks forward to another on positive psychology.

Health Behavior

Brenda maintains a healthy lifestyle. She's current on her health checkups. On sunny days, she walks or jogs on a nearby bike path. She also attends yoga and Zumba classes organized by the company's wellness program. Brenda is a strong role model of healthy fitness for all employees.

Purpose

Brenda feels she can utilize her people skills in her human resources job. She's always been a great listener. She's finding many problems can be sorted out just by getting valuable information and involving each team in coming up with reasonable solutions. She finds this empowerment approach meaningful.

Brenda is also pleased about taking on a leadership role within the company, breaking the glass ceiling for woman at the executive level. She hopes to give woman equal voice in what had been a male-dominated organization.

Brenda is delighted she can now pay for her children's college tuition, a big weight off her shoulders.

Brenda is uncomfortable making some human resource policies designed to maximize profits. Most recently, the company installed an online cash register system. Headquarters gets an immediate tally used to make staffing decisions at the local level. If sales are slow, the store manager is instructed to send employees home. Brenda knows this is hard on employees and their store managers; many employees navigate long commutes, must pay for childcare, and can't afford to work less. Brenda is embarrassed about enforcing such harsh working conditions.

José Rodriguez, Machine Operator

José recently moved from his hometown of Queretaro, Mexico to join his cousin Juan in Santa Clara, California. Billings Tool and Die Company operates a plant in both locations. Juan told José they paid twice as much in California, and the company needed machine operators. José was skilled at his job, having interned in Queretaro right out of high school. Now in his late twenties, he could create tools, parts, and objects by operating milling and drilling machines, grinders, and lathes in a machine shop. The work is extremely precise, requiring him to make cuts to at least one-thousandth of an inch. The equipment and responsibilities in Queretaro were nearly the same as those in Santa Clara. He turned raw metal into useful equipment.

Safety

For many immigrants the biggest challenge is obtaining legal status in the United States. Fortunately, for José, Billings Tool and Die Company got him a green card. Unlike many of his new friends and neighbors, José is safe from arrest and deportation. Still, he knows he is always suspect and can be temporarily detained without warning.

The biggest safety hazard is not at work, but at home. Juan and José live in a rough neighborhood; gun shots ring out in the night and sirens are heard at all hours. This is what they can afford.

José also has trouble with his immediate manager and the corporate office. Neither his immediate supervisor nor the human resources department people speak Spanish. He could tell they want him to do things but must ask for a translation from his coworkers, making communication far from perfect. José only gleans the basic gist of what is being said, and the likelihood he is missing something important makes him anxious.

Presence

Like many immigrants, José misses his friends and family, thinking of them often. He dreams of returning to Queretaro flush with cash and ready to start a family.

José does not feel comfortable in a gathering where English is spoken, making it difficult for him to relax in most social situations. To relax, he drinks a beer while watching sports on Spanish television.

Connections

José's primary support system is a thousand miles away in Queretaro. His cousin, Juan, is his primary local connection. He calls his parents once a week. They seem so far away. He misses the warm friendly greeting he always got in his hometown, "*Buenos diaz.*"

José has a couple friends at work, all from his hometown, Queretaro. He feels an immediate bond, as they possess very similar life stories. These coworkers invited him to join them for a local church service. He's hopeful he will meet more people at church.

Adaptability

José always viewed himself as mentally tough. Mexican men carry a macho tradition that features an external show of strength. Inside, however, José has a lot happening "under the hood." In private moments, José cries. Adapting to life in California isn't easy. Learning English and fitting in is a high priority.

Health Behavior

José is not exercising. It's not safe to walk anywhere near his home, especially at night. Juan and José commute at least an hour each way to work, leaving little time for exercise. They can't afford anything closer to their workplace in Santa Clara. He wants to fit in. Real Californians drive, even if the destination is just around the corner.

The shop floor is often close to 100 degrees. The vending machines feature Coke products. José wishes the company would provide cold drinking water.

José has not seen a doctor or a dentist since leaving Mexico. Language and lack of time are barriers. He's also heard that health care is expensive. The company offers insurance, but there is a deductible.

Purpose

José came to California to make money. Mission accomplished. He likes his new salary, but everything feels like a sacrifice. He misses his large family gatherings, his church, and even the friendly faces of Queretaro. He dreams of finding love and having children but does not see how that would work in California.

José likes his work and is good at it, making parts to be assembled elsewhere into finished products he's only seen in pictures. José does not feel any connection to the company and what it makes. He has never met an actual customer.

Chapter 3

Align Cultural Support with Proactive Mental Health

"Some seeds fell by the wayside, and the fowls came and devoured them up; some fell upon stony places... and because they had no root, they withered away. And some fell among thorns and the thorns sprung up, and choked them: but others, fell into good ground, and brought forth fruit..."

—MATTHEW 13: 4-8

CULTURE, AN ABSTRACT idea for many people, is a complex web of social influences on attitudes and behaviors. The word, *culture*, has its origins in the farming concept of cultivation. Just like farming practices, groups and organizations can work to align social influences so that effective ideas, such as proactive mental health, can take root and grow. Most team cultures harbor subcultures. The most common subcultures form around job responsibilities, managers, departments, shifts, races, genders, and work locations. In the new hybrid work schedules, household, friends, and family subcultures take on added importance, as part of the culture web also.

Although the strands of the culture web are intertwined, taking a closer look at primary cultural influences—the culture building blocks— can bring culture into focus. Each influence also represents an opportunity for supporting important goals, such as proactive mental health.

Figure 2. Culture Building Blocks

Social Climate

Social climate—closely associated with collaboration, morale, teamwork, synergy and overall work atmosphere—is both the glue and the lubricant within a culture. There are three primary social climate factors: positive outlook, shared vision, and sense of community.

Sense of Community

Figure 3. Social Climate Factors

1. A sense of community whereby people trust one another, care for one another in times of need, feel belonging, and get to know one another.

2. A shared vision whereby people see that their values are represented, feel inspired about what the organization is doing, and see how they contribute to overall success.

3. A positive outlook whereby people recognize strengths and accomplishments, have a "can do attitude," tackle difficult challenges with enthusiasm and have fun together.

Many strategies for strengthening the work climate required face-to-face interactions. It is highly likely this culture dimension has been undermined by pandemic-induced changes such as working from home. Most of the mechanisms for strengthening the work climate need a serious rethink and revitalization. Strategies for measuring and strengthening the social climate are the focus of Chapter 3.

Culture Questions

1. What do we do now to strengthen all three work climate factors?
2. How will we supplement and/or replace our old approach to building community, fostering a shared vision, and maintaining a positive work atmosphere?

Shared Values

While we often think of values on a personal level, cultures also shape and accommodate values. They are sometimes called "priorities." Typical values in successful organizations include: (1) care for the well-being of employees, (2) customer service, (3) productivity, and (4) innovation.

Sometimes value conflicts undermine the culture. Equity is one of the values causing a lot of conflict. This is a long-standing and unresolved concern. Women are often paid less than men for similar work. Some executives are compensated at a level out of line with the efforts of other hard-working employees.

Culture Questions

1. What are our primary corporate values and how might they need to be strengthened or changed?

2. How will we demonstrate our commitment to these values?

3. What value conflicts need to be resolved and how?

Norms

Norms are social expectations about attitudes and behavior, often recognized (or disguised) as, "The way we do things around here." Norms influence everything from language and safety practices to work style. They frequently shadow us as an invisible force we get used to. This is called *acculturation.*

Since a group's norms are contextually informative and socially meaningful, hopefully, your team possesses many norms that support your success, such as coming to work rested. Unfortunately, many teams have norms that undermine health and productivity. In some teams, for example, there are few boundaries between work time and home time. The norm is to work 24/7. Chapter 6 includes an assessment of common proactive mental health norm goals.

Culture Questions

1. What are our norm strengths and how will we keep them going now?

2. What new norms are needed to address current work conditions?

Touchpoints

Touchpoints are numerous informal and formal day-to-day influences on behavior and attitudes. Chapter 6 offers definitions of the primary touchpoints and discusses how touchpoints can be aligned with proactive mental health.

Cultural Touchpoints

1. Resource Commitment
2. Built Environment
3. Communication and Information
4. Rewards and Recognition
5. Relationship Development (Make it Social)
6. Learning and Training
7. Modeling
8. Pushback
9. Onboarding
10. Traditions and Symbols
11. Story and Narrative
12. Roles and Responsibilities
13. Goal Setting and Planning
14. Laws and Policies

Cultural touchpoints are like cultural norms in that we get accustomed to them. You may not be sharply aware day to day, but touchpoints are already hard at work in your organization. Your goal is to better align them with your culture goals. You need not shift all the touchpoints to strengthen a new norm or value, but you need to reach a tipping point of day-to-day influences. What follows is an example of how touchpoints might be used to support a norm for adequate sleep.

Built Environment	Provide a quiet place at work suitable for resting. Assist with the redesign of household bedrooms for quality sleep.
Resource Commitment	Modify work schedules so they are consistent hours from week to week.
Learning and Training	Provide education on proper sleep hygiene, sleep cycles and adequate sleep.
Communication and Information	Track aggregate results gathered from sleep journals and post regular updates.
Reward and Recognize	Celebrate increases in the percentage of employees reporting good sleep practices.
Modeling	For team leaders to keep sleep journals and share how they are doing with their sleep goals.

Culture Questions

1. What are our current touchpoint strengths and how will we maintain and build upon them?

2. What touchpoints will need to be realigned to reinforce desirable norms?

Peer Support

Peer support is assistance provided by coworkers, friends, family, and neighbors, such as the loaning of tools and equipment and covering for childcare. Peer support also comes in the form of emotional assistance, such as sympathy and being present. Peer support is beneficial for both the person giving and receiving support. Providing peer support raises self-esteem and builds someone's social network. Those receiving peer support are much more likely to maintain desired personal changes. Chapter 4 teaches eight primary peer support skills, designed to increase the quantity and quality of peer support for personal proactive mental health goals.

Culture Questions

1. Do employees have sufficient opportunities to help one another?

2. How can we strengthen the quality and quantity of peer support provided by coworkers, friends, family, and the community?

Leadership Support

Executives, managers, and peer leaders can lower barriers and enhance policies and practices that support health and productivity. If you are reading this book, it is likely you are one of these leaders. There are six primary ways leaders influence the culture:

1. Share the proactive mental health vision including what the new culture will look like, why it is important, and how people can contribute to the effort.
2. Serve as role models for desired change.
3. Build a plan for culture change.
4. Strengthen the work climate.
5. Align touchpoints with culture goals.
6. Track and celebrate individual and team achievements.

Culture Questions

1. Who will lead this culture initiative?
2. How will we empower leaders to perform the six leadership responsibilities?

The Power of Culture in Proactive Mental Health

Proactive mental health is achieved through attitudes and behavior that prevent mental illness and enhance mental well-being. Little is achieved if people are unable to change unhealthy practices and maintain positive practices. So, for example, an employee interested in strengthening social connections (a proactive mental health building block) needs to spend quality time interacting with coworkers, family, and friends. An employee seeking to achieve financial security (safety is a proactive mental health building block) may need to follow through on financial planning and adhering to a household budget. Another employee seeking to avoid depression may seek to achieve daily physical activity.

There is strong evidence that health behavior change initiatives are unlikely to achieve their potential due to unsupportive cultural environments. In unsupportive cultures now commonplace, most people are unable to achieve their personal health goals. Why? Making a lasting change in behavior is rarely a simple process. It usually involves a substantial commitment of time, effort, and emotion— all that run smoother with the backdrop of peer support. Although personal commitment and attention are important to initiate a behavior change, when personal attention turns to other priorities, cultural support is needed to maintain the change. Most people are ready to change, but continual follow-through is elusive without an accountability partner or at least an informed and reassuring group.

Unsupportive cultures are the primary reasons why behavior change is only temporary, as people quickly revert to normal practice. Twenty percent is a reasonable stretch goal for success rates in well-designed programs. People tend to revert to their base-line behaviors soon after their participation in a program ends. Cultural influences overwhelm positive intentions and new skills. This problem persists across the spectrum of health behavior goals (e.g., physical, social, and psychological).

Each culture building block provides opportunities to support proactive mental health. You and your employees can align the organizational culture with proactive mental health. Just as importantly, your culture change skills will make it possible for you to address unforeseen future challenges and opportunities. The culture change approach will make it possible for you to continuously co-create workplace cultures that match your team's responsibilities and support the well-being of each employee. Not an easy assignment, but very worthwhile.

Assessing Your Team's Proactive Mental Health Culture

Due to the complexity and invisibility of culture (seen with acculturation), measurement is an important step to devising a culture change strategy. One approach is to bring in an outside expert observer to provide an independent and fresh perspective. Another measurement strategy is to conduct interviews and focus groups to discover how cultural building blocks are influencing proactive mental health. A third strategy is to conduct an employee culture survey. The following survey provides a snapshot of the six culture building blocks. Additional survey tools for more granular measures of a single building block are available in the *We Flourish* chapters on social climate and cultural norms.

Proactive Mental Health Culture Survey

Proactive mental health is a combination of attitudes and behaviors that prevent mental illness and support overall mental well-being. Proactive mental health includes such things as being able to be present, to adapt, and to connect with others. It is also about being economically, physically, and socially safe. Proactive mental health includes doing things that provide meaning and purpose. In addition, it includes healthy lifestyle practices such as physical activity, healthy eating and avoiding alcohol and other drug addictions.

The following confidential and anonymous survey measures the level of cultural support for proactive mental health attitudes and behaviors. You are being asked about the culture among the people you work most closely with. Your opinions count even if your answers indicate that the culture is not sending clear signals. Your "undecided/don't know" answer also helps when it comes to measuring the impact of the culture.

Note: There are no incorrect answers. We are asking for your opinion. If the question does not apply to your work environment, select NA for Not Applicable.

Instructions: *Using the five-point scale, rate your level of agreement with the following statements.*

5 strongly agree

4 Agree

3 Neither agree nor disagree / neutral

2 Disagree

1 Strongly disagree

NA Not applicable

Leadership	
My immediate supervisor supports my efforts to adopt attitudes and behaviors that support my proactive mental health (see definition above).	5 4 3 2 1 NA
My immediate supervisor models good proactive mental health practices.	5 4 3 2 1 NA
Shared Values	
In my team, we care about the mental health of employees.	5 4 3 2 1 NA
Supporting employee proactive mental health is among the top priorities in my team.	5 4 3 2 1 NA
Peer Support	
My immediate coworkers support one another's efforts to achieve proactive mental health (for example, coworkers would support efforts to reduce unsafe living or working conditions).	5 4 3 2 1 NA

Using the five-point scale, rate your level agreement with the following statements

My organization has initiatives that encourage employees to work together to develop and maintain their proactive mental health (for example, joining together for fitness activities or to practice yoga).	5 4 3 2 1 NA
Touchpoints	
Proactive mental health is supported by aspects of the physical work environment (for example, we have healthy food options, there are places to relax, and it is a safe place to work).	5 4 3 2 1 NA
In my team, proactive mental health behaviors are recognized and rewarded (for example, people who achieve work-life balance, get fit, and eat healthy are likely to be praised for their efforts).	5 4 3 2 1 NA
Norms	
It is expected and accepted in your immediate team to get help with mental health problems early on.	5 4 3 2 1 NA
It is expected and accepted in your immediate team to pursue at least one proactive mental health goal (such as to eat or sleep better).	5 4 3 2 1 NA

Social Climate	
In my team, we have a sense of community (for example, people get to know one another, feel as if they belong, and care for one another in times of need).	5 4 3 2 1 NA
In my team, there is a positive outlook (for example, we enjoy our work, celebrate our accomplishments, and adopt a "we can do it" attitude).	5 4 3 2 1 NA
In my team, there is a shared vision (for example, we find work inspiring, we have resolved values conflicts, and work is done in a way that is consistent with our values).	5 4 3 2 1 NA

Scoring Your Culture Survey

The most accurate findings would be achieved by including responses from all your co-workers. However, average scores for your responses present an indication of the level of cultural support for proactive mental health in your team. An average above 4 represents a strong proactive mental health culture. If your average score is close to 3, your culture is not sending clear signals in support of proactive mental health. Hopefully, you have many existing strengths to build upon. Most organizations also afford plenty of opportunities for improvement. This illuminating snapshot is a place to begin.

Your Role in Creating Supportive Cultural Environments

Culture need not be forced on any individual or group. Fortunately, most people are already in favor of supporting mental health. If not, you can build the case by calling attention to the many advantages of reducing mental illness and supporting mental well-being. In most workplaces, you can turn your attention to co-creating the proactive mental health culture people want and need.

Increase the Quantity and Quality of Peer Support

"If you want to lift yourself up, lift up someone else."

– BOOKER T. WASHINGTON

SUSTAINED CHANGE IN daily behavior is often difficult to achieve. A lot more can be accomplished with support from a coworker, immediate supervisor, friend, family member, or neighbor. Effective peer support for proactive mental health has four qualities that set it apart from other forms of informal and non-paid support:

- Creating a safe and caring relationship for exploring mental health goals. This requires establishing trust and working to keep communications open, positive, and guilt-free.

- Asking questions useful in planning personal change. Doing more listening than telling. Asking for clarification and reflecting upon what is heard, often referred to as active listening. Those engaged in effective support are more likely to offer more thought-provoking questions than advice.

- Seeking out resources for achieving your peer's goals. You utilize your contacts and ingenuity to discover useful information and to gain needed resources. You may, for instance, join your peer in talking with someone who has achieved similar goals, web surfing, or attending a seminar. You may also brainstorm strategies for freeing time for pursuing goals.

- Embracing the learning and growth that come from someone's journey. Your primary concern is avoiding negative judgments and instead, supporting your peer in taking heartfelt actions truly reflecting personal choice.

Your role is different from professional support roles; you will not be compensated financially for your help. Whereas a counselor or therapist is focused on the deeper psychological causes underlying a behavior, you focus on the practical aspects of health behavior change. You may help your peer find a counselor if deeper and more mysterious problems need attention.

Although teachers and personal coaches are professionals who guide people with their expertise in a particular area, you are not claiming to be a counseling or health expert. You will ask questions designed to guide your peer toward determining their own best direction, rather than saying what you think is the best direction. You will join forces in seeking out useful information from reliable sources.

Peer Support Skill #1: Establishing a Solid Foundation for Effective Peer Support

Furnishing effective peer support is sometimes known as *mentoring*, with its origins in Homer's *The Odyssey*. Odysseus, king of Ithaca, was leaving to fight in the Trojan War and needed someone who could help his independent-minded son Telemachus learn to be a king. Odysseus chose a man named Mentor because he possessed special skills. Recognizing his personal experiences would have limited value, Mentor taught by asking questions and learning through personal exploration. In this way, Mentor encouraged Telemachus to pursue his natural inclinations and to change directions based on that learning. Mentor's strategy worked. Telemachus went on to become a helpful son and leader.

As in *The Odyssey*, offering effective peer support does not require direct personal experience with a particular goal. Instead, it occurs through the mutual embrace of the learning and growth of a personal wellness journey. Assistance comes primarily in the form of thought-provoking questions rather than advice. You recognize that knowledge unfolds during the process of change. The mentor has faith that the peer can, and most often will, find the best path to wellness.

Establishing Trust

Supporting successful proactive mental health goals usually requires a high level of trust. There are four primary ways peers establish and maintain trust. The four "Cs" of trust are:

- Contextual Trust
- Communication Trust
- Contractual Trust
- Competence Trust

Contextual Trust

Contextual trust means that our relationship with our peer carries a broad basis of familiarity. As we get to know the history and special interests of others, we can begin to appreciate and trust them more. Sometimes this form of trust is established through years of shared life experiences. This could be true of family members or longtime friends. However, all too often, people spend years working and living side by side without really knowing very much about the other's range of experiences. Thus, at work, we may be aware of a peer's specific task or job responsibility without knowing anything about her family life, hobbies, and personal aspirations.

When pondering contextual trust, think about the relationship-building skills of successful salespeople. A successful salesperson, sitting down with a customer, does not immediately make sales pitches unless the customer insists.

Instead, he opens with a discussion of common personal interests such as hobbies, family responsibilities or sports. He builds trust before negotiating the best business deal. In a similar way, we should not leap into giving or getting support for health behavior change. First, establish a relationship.

By broadening the basis of a relationship, we will feel more comfortable expressing our true feelings and be better able to give and receive constructive feedback and the person receiving the feedback is more likely to experience feedback as having been given in the spirit of helpfulness. In contrast, if all we know about a person is related to one unhealthy behavior, then feedback about that behavior often feels like a criticism of the whole person. When constructive suggestions or probing questions are offered in the context of a broad relationship, it's less likely to feel like a criticism.

Communication Trust

The second "C" of trust, communication trust, refers to the willingness to disclose relevant information, to be truthful, and to using your peer's personal information in a considerate way. When it comes to giving and receiving support for lasting behavior change, accurate and complete information is essential. If you withhold your true feelings, the quality and quantity of support is undermined. In contrast, when communication trust is high, information flows freely. There are five key concepts that build—or detract from—your communication trust:

Confidentiality Agreements

Agreements about privacy help build trust by outlining how and when personal information may be shared with others. When you are supporting a health behavior goal, there will be times when it could be useful to collect input from outside sources. To maintain communication trust, you must share information only in a way that has been previously agreed to.

Establish your confidentiality guidelines early. Start with broad guidelines and then adjust if unanticipated situations arise. The following guidelines will help you get started. You may want to add a couple of special situations in which personal beliefs, rules, or laws dictate the disclosure of information. For example, if you are working with a school bus driver, you might want to state up front that if the conversation indicates alcohol or drugs are being used at work, you will find it necessary to contact the employee assistance program or other authorities for assistance. Discuss such limitations on confidentiality in advance. The following guidelines are a reliable starting place. You may need to add conditions, as the example of helping a school bus driver shows.

Suggested Confidentiality Guidelines

- *I recognize my ability to provide support depends on your confidence and trust in me.*
- *I recognize what you tell me is in confidence.*

- *I will not disclose anything you tell me to anyone without first getting your permission, unless you say you are planning to physically harm yourself or someone else.*

- *I will never use the information you give me against you in any way.*

The Concept of Need to Know

Contextual trust is helpful in getting to know each other. However, there are aspects of people's lives that should remain private. Where possible, confine your questioning and probing to relevant information. Encourage your peer to keep conversations focused on wellness goals. Keeping communication purposeful and on topic will help maintain communication trust.

The Obligation to Disclose

Withholding pertinent information or giving false information undermines communication trust. When it comes to behavior change, slips and setbacks can feel embarrassing. Most hunches and feelings are better disclosed and are usually worth exploring even if they are unfounded. Even when information is unflattering, tell the whole truth. Explain yourself fully. Working through hunches and feelings is a good way to establish and maintain trust.

Acknowledging Misunderstandings and Mistakes

A certain amount of trial and error accompanies innovation. At some point, you will misinterpret, not communicate well, or be misunderstood. Acknowledge such errors, apologize, explain what you have learned, and work toward new understanding. In most situations, little value is gained focusing or dwelling on mistakes, but acknowledge such errors before moving on. Acknowledgement builds trust and enables you to move forward with a minimum of residual baggage.

Attentive Listening

The way we listen enhances or undermines communication trust. The person speaking needs to feel heard and you want your input to begiven thoughtful consideration. You can accomplish this by looking at the person speaking, asking for clarification, and paraphrasing what is being said to be sure you fully understand. Bring your focus to what is being said. Try to avoid jumping to conclusions or judging before your peer has an opportunity to fully explain and you have had a chance to digest the information. It's okay to offer your initial reactions but acknowledge these are, in fact, first impressions and not any thorough conclusions. Open your mind to your peer's way of seeing things. Offer your perspective in the spirit of kindness, mutual acceptance and the desire to be truly helpful.

Contractual Trust

Contractual trust, the third "C," is developed when peers come to agreement about how their relationship will function. This doesn't mean that rules are set in stone, but it does mean that the helping relationship will be organized in a way that respects time and other commitments. For example, it is important to establish how often to discuss the peer support goal. You may also need to consider how long you will continue to discuss the goal before you will adjust or end your conversations. Maintaining a schedule, sticking with it, and showing up on time are all examples of how to build contractual trust.

Contractual trust includes full disclosure of any benefits or compensation. You should explain why you are offering assistance.

The reason can be as straightforward as the desire to help. If you are assisting because you have received similar help in the past, telling that story is likely to build contractual trust. If you are seeking to develop skills for a future career in the helping professions, that should be disclosed. Any form of anticipated compensation should be disclosed.

Competence Trust

The final "C," competence trust, involves respecting people's knowledge, skills, abilities, and judgments. To establish this form of trust, you must be clear about your strengths and limitations. For example, you should let your peer know if you have little formal training or experience with an issue that has been raised. An offer of support should not be mistaken for a declaration that you know a great deal about your peer's goals and how they are best achieved. Frank disclosure of experience (or the lack thereof) enhances competence trust.

It is not enough to declare a lack of familiarity, knowledgeor skills. You can build trust by accompanying your peer to a library, bookstore, or other information source to get needed information. You will build competence trust by actively pursuing useful information.

Peer Support Skill #2: Help with Goal Setting

The proactive mental health self-assessment introduced in Chapter 2 provides an effective starting place for a conversation about possible goals. You and your peer can use these questions to begin a conversation about setting proactive mental health goals. It bears repeating here to underscore Peer Support for Proactive Mental Health.

Proactive Mental Health Self-Assessment

Proactive mental health is a constellation of 26 behaviors and attitudes that prevent mental illness and increase overall mental well-being. The following confidential proactive mental health self-assessment asks about your current practices and about the importance of each practice to your mental health. Your answers will help prioritize efforts to support mental health.

Instructions: *Using the five-point scale, rate how consistently you experience the proactive mental health attitudes and behaviors.*

5 Always
4 Often
3 Sometimes
2 Rarely
1 Never
NA Not applicable

How are you doing this week?

ATTITUDES AND BEHAVIOR	Current Practice
Presence	
Are you able to focus on the here-and-now?	5 4 3 2 1 NA
Do you declutter and destress your life so you can experience inner peace?	5 4 3 2 1 NA
Do you practice daily stress management techniques such as taking a walk, meditation, or yoga?	5 4 3 2 1 NA
Connection	
Are you able to love and be loved?	5 4 3 2 1 NA
Do you spend time with friends most days?	5 4 3 2 1 NA
Can you forgive?	5 4 3 2 1 NA
Are you grateful?	5 4 3 2 1 NA
Can you trust others and are you trustworthy?	5 4 3 2 1 NA
Are you good at teamwork?	5 4 3 2 1 NA

ATTITUDES AND BEHAVIOR	Current Practice
Adaptability	
Can you handle disappointment?	5 4 3 2 1 NA
Do you persist in the face of challenges?	5 4 3 2 1 NA
Are you open to trying new ways of doing things?	5 4 3 2 1 NA
Do you consider your strengths before taking on tasks and challenges?	5 4 3 2 1 NA
Do you avoid seeing problems or bad news as permanent, pervasive (affecting all things), or personal (about you)?	5 4 3 2 1 NA
Purpose	
Do you feel like you are making a difference?	5 4 3 2 1 NA
Do you regularly do things that give your life meaning?	5 4 3 2 1 NA
Do you experience passion and commitment?	5 4 3 2 1 NA
Safety	
Do you feel economically secure?	5 4 3 2 1 NA
Are you free from physical and emotional violence and abuse?	5 4 3 2 1 NA
Do you live, work, and play in healthy physical environments?	5 4 3 2 1 NA
Health Behavior	
Are you current on your preventive medical health screenings?	5 4 3 2 1 NA
Do you get help with mental and physical health problems early on?	5 4 3 2 1 NA
Do you eat a healthy diet?	5 4 3 2 1 NA
Are you free from addictions to alcohol and other drugs?	5 4 3 2 1 NA
Do you get adequate rest?	5 4 3 2 1 NA

Review your responses. How are you doing with your proactive mental health? You can be mentally healthy without achieving all 26 practices. Most people completing this questionnaire identify both personal strengths and opportunities for improvement.

Help your peer to set short- and long-term proactive mental health goals. You two can even do some research on what the experts say are reasonable goals. Mental health professionals, books, journals and even a respected website can be helpful in thinking about short- and long-term goals.

Spark the conversation by asking your peer to describe current plans for personal change. If multiple goals are mentioned, ask about which goals to start with.

Most behavior change goals are achieved in stages. The process often begins with developing commitment to change and ends with having a change so firmly in place that setbacks are no longer likely. Many of us are somewhere in the middle of this process. Work with your peer to identify the current stages of change to help focus on the most meaningful steps now.

Sometimes the personal change process is not clear. Added clarity helps break complex changes into achievable actions. It also increases accountability. James Prochaska and Carlo DiClemente's created a useful behavior change roadmap that is incorporated into the following table. Talk with your peer to help identify progress and to set the short- and long-term goals that are most meaningful now.

A Road Map for Personal Change

	Stage of Change	Appropriate Change Goal
1	**DEVELOPING COMMITMENT:** Your peer is not truly convinced about the importance of the lifestyle goal. Your peer may be just exploring the general possibility of taking on a particular goal. For example, someone might have told him such a goal is worthwhile.	If you find yourselves in the "exploratory phase," then the goal is to get more information about the value of such a change.
2.	**CONTEMPLATION:** Your peer would like to change and thinks they are likely to attempt change in the next six months.	Your peer should set a date for making the change. Engaging in conversation about the possibilities can often help solidify your thinking.

3.	**PREPARATION:** Your peer is planning to take action in the immediate future (usually within the next month) and is determining the best strategy to carry out the change.	Together, develop the plan for how the change will be carried out. Your peer should let others know about the intention to change.
4.	**ACTION:** Your peer is engaged in making changes.	Help your peer adjust to the new lifestyle and manage unexpected emotional and physical reactions.
5.	**MAINTENANCE:** Your peer is working to integrate the behavior change into her normal day-to-day life.	Continue to pay attention to the behavior and work through any relapse. The central focus for your peer is to get comfortable with the new behavior and have it become fully integrated into other aspects of life. Your peer can also mentor someone with similar goals. Teaching tends to reinforce positive changes.

| 6. | MOVING ON: Your peer has maintained the change for a year or more and has not been tempted by the old behavior. | Help your peer set new health-enhancing goals. Move on from support systems that are focused exclusively on the prior goal. It is no longer useful for your peer to look at himself as one step from relapse. It's time to move on to other goals and interests. |

These stages of change are not a fixed or necessary process. Sometimes people just put their mind to something and the change clicks into place. However, discussing the stages can be very useful in setting both current, intermediate, and long-term goals, and help determining the most appropriate support. For instance, if someone is already making change, a conversation about why to change may not be well received or necessary. The decision as has already been made.

Peer Support Skill #3: Help Identify a Role Model

Once proactive mental health goals are set, you can help your peer by finding a good role model to talk with. When it comes to personal changes, the most effective role model is likely to be someone who has successfully achieved a similar goal under similar circumstances. Such a role model can share lessons learned through personal experience:

- A role model is likely to be knowledgeable about where to go for quality information about the proactive mental health goal.

- A role model can explain how to measure success along the way. For example, maybe there were small goals that added up to a larger change.

- A role model can explain how to stay on track and how barriers or setbacks were overcome.

- A role model can discuss how peers helped make the change possible.

Talk with your peer about how to find a suitable role model. Who has achieved a similar goal under comparable circumstances? Ideally, the role model would be someone one or both of you already know and be someone your peer can actually get in touch with. Sometimes finding such a person takes a little digging. Are there people working in mental health, wellness, and human resources who might provide a role model referral? Are there books, magazine articles, or movies featuring a possible role model? Does someone in your social network know a role model? A little brainstorming may reveal some likely places to start your search.

Peer Support Skill #4: Help Eliminate Barriers to Change

Successful personal change requires resources such as time, tools and equipment, and focus. Where they are noticeably absent, these resources become barriers to success. Ask your peer to identify or determine which resources they need to be successful.

Time is a common concern. Ask about possible time constraints. How much time is needed? Is there a regular time slot available? Is there another way to cover responsibilities or combine these responsibilities with other tasks? For example, one parent with a goal to exercise more found they could walk around the soccer field during practice. Could someone else pick up some responsibilities such as childcare to free up time to pursue your proactive mental health goal? Would a manager or spouse give permission to use a more flexible schedule to accommodate this effort and new lifestyle practice?

Skills and equipment are often helpful. Ask about the availability of these resources. Is there a comfortable, safe, affordable, and convenient place to do this practice? Ideally, your peer would become skilled at doing the proactive mental health behavior. What instruction and expert advice is available? What clothing and equipment are needed? How will this be acquired?

Willpower plays a decisive role in most lifestyle changes. Talk with your peer about focus. How easy will it be to stay focused and committed? What is their experience with willpower? What lessons can be learned from the past? What would strengthen accountability? For example, a sleep journal could help keep a plan for regular sleep on track. What mental health strategies will be helpful? For example, getting regular sleep, daily meditation and establishing pleasant routines create a more decluttered mindset. If willpower will be a large issue, a therapist or counselor could also help work through some more deeply rooted psychological barriers.

Conduct a strengths review. Our strengths help us move forward. Talk to your peer about personal strengths and other available assets. What successes have been achieved in the past? What lessons can be learned from these positive experiences? What resources are already available? Who is likely to be helpful? What personal values and motivations are likely to help with willpower?

Peer Support Skill #5: Locate Supportive Environments

Over the long haul, physical and social environments can make or break our efforts to make changes. You can help identify the people and places that will be most supportive to your peer's success. Your peer can reduce exposure to less supportive people and places.

Take an inventory of the key environments at home, at work, and in the neighborhood or community. What are they? Every person holds a different mix. Many people now work at home. Some people spend a lot of time with extended family. Others are often visiting friends or frequent a favorite bar or restaurant.

When contemplating each of these key environments, what level of support is likely? The goal is to avoid less supportive places and spend more time in places where the healthy choice is the easy choice.

Norms play integral roles in supporting positive health practices. Is the new healthy lifestyle practice normal and expected or would it be ridiculed? Some groups lack a cultural preference, meaning they would be neutral and not send clear signals one way another. Could people agree to keep their unhealthy behavior out of sight or in another location, for example? How could we increase time among groups where the new healthy practice is a strong norm? In such settings, almost all people are already practicing the desired behavior or at least aspiring to achieve the same healthy goal.

Social climate is another important consideration. When people are embroiled in conflict or can't find middle ground, it is difficult to focus and obtain needed support. Three social climate factors enhance the capacity for people to change.

- How would your peer rate personal environments in terms of **sense of community?** Do people get to know each other? Do people trust one another? Does your peer feel a sense of belonging? Note that belonging is highly correlated to engagement.

- How would your peer rate personal environments in terms of a **positive atmosphere?** Do people laugh? Are they optimistic? Do people celebrate accomplishments? Do people avoid focusing exclusively on what's wrong? Do people resolve conflicts?

- How would your peer rate personal environments in terms of a **shared vision?** Are people inspired? Do people share values in common? Are people working in alignment? Are there clear shared purposes?

The physical environment also plays an important role

in sustaining personal changes. Are there ways physical environments could be made more supportive of your peer's goal? Could more time be spent in nearby parks, bike paths and recreational facilities? Could the proactive mental health goal be a factor in planning vacations? Could new equipment or a rearrangement of physical space help? Some people purchase blackout curtains for their bedrooms or purchase home fitness equipment. Other people change their workstation so that they can stand or even walk.

Peer Support Skill #6: Help Work Through or Avoid Setbacks

Personal change efforts can get off track. Getting back on track often requires support. The embarrassment and guilt associated with getting off track can undermine supportive relationships. You can have proactive conversations with your peer to prevent this communication breakdown. Anticipate high-risk situations so some setbacks will be avoided.

Share your feelings about setbacks without giving your peer the impression that such setbacks are inevitable.

Here are some tips:

- It's best to get back on track soon after the slip or relapse. This leads to a conversation about "incident" rather than an argument or debate about an ongoing defeat. Agree to check-in regularly just to see how things are going.

- Discuss high-risk situations and devise strategies for reducing their impact. For example, air travel and airports are not conducive places for getting exercise. Planning ahead, such as doing yoga or taking a walk first, can make this less of a problem. Family holidays are also notorious for disrupting healthy behavior. Setting reasonable goals for such challenging times can reduce the psychological setback.

- If a setback occurs, try to avoid conversations that would be more appropriate between a guilty child and parent. As a peer, your job is to collect the facts, determine where things stand, and give your peer an adult role in determining where things go from here.

- Remind your peer the setback does not invalidate past personal successes. Without sounding like you are avoiding the current situation, conduct a review of your peer's strengths and resources.

- Encourage your peer to reach out to a role model for recommendations on how to deal with setbacks.

- Recommend your peer spend more time in supportive physical and social environments.

- Maybe some additional resources of time, knowledge, equipment, and skills could make the difference in getting back on track. Help your peer address resource barriers to change.

Peer Support Skill #7: Help Celebrate Progress

Celebrating is an enjoyable and rewarding form of peer support. Unfortunately, many successes go unacknowledged. Positive feedback is a compelling reward, and celebrating progress is helpful for staying on track. The following techniques will help you and your peer to celebrate progress:

- Break goals into intermediate steps. Celebrate when these intermediate benchmarks are achieved.

- Recognize dates of accomplishment. For example, an alcoholic might celebrate months and then years of sobriety.

- Ask your peer about his or her preferences related to public disclosure. Some people prefer a quiet and anonymous celebration. Others dream of a party. Match the celebration to your peer's preferences.

- Determine the best celebrants. Your peer is likely to have personal preferences of who they might celebrate with. Sometimes it is a specific family member. For some people, recognition by coworkers or managers would be most important.

- Try to select rewards consistent with the accomplishment. A gift card for a natural foods market might be best for a person pursuing a healthier diet.

- Include group celebrations. When possible, and if your peer is comfortable with it, honor what people have achieved together. This approach could include honoring a peer's support network.

Reviewing Key Ideas about Providing Effective Peer Support

The purpose of peer support is to assist a coworker, friend, or family member to achieve their proactive mental health goals. Friends, family, and coworkers are in a unique position to provide the ongoing support needed to achieve lasting change. Many people do not provide the level of effective peer support to help someone achieve lasting personal changes. One way to improve the quantity and quality of peer support is to: (1) establish a solid foundation by being clear about the peer support role and by developing trust, (2) help set goals, (3) help identify good role models, (4) help eliminate barriers to change, (5) help locate supportive environments, (6) help avoid or work through setbacks, and (7) help celebrate progress.

Chapter 5

Improve the Social Climate

"Alone we can do so little; together we can do so much."

—Helen Keller

Social climate is the dimension of culture related to social cohesiveness and teamwork. Other words for social climate are *social capital*, *high morale*, *teamwork*, and *conviviality*. Social climate fulfills roles in several dimensions of proactive mental health including adaptability, presence, and connections. When people don't get along, it is difficult to follow through on personal mental health goals. In contrast, in groups where there is high morale and positive energy, proactive mental health is easier to achieve.

When people don't get along, they are less likely to relax, think clearly, and enjoy life. The research supporting the health benefits of positive social connections are among the most conclusive in the social sciences. President and founder of the nonprofit Preventive Medicine Research Institute Dr. Dean Ornish summarized his review of more than 100 studies: "I am not aware of any other factor in medicine—not diet, not smoking, not exercise, not stress, not genetics, not drugs, not surgery—that has a greater impact on our quality of life, incidence of illness, and pre-mature death from all causes."

Social climate uniquely creates conditions for both individual well-being and organizational growth. Don Cohen and Laurence Pursak offer a comprehensive review of this supportive literature in their groundbreaking book, *In Good Company: How Social Capital Makes Organizations Work*. These Harvard Business School authors identified four core primary benefits. Favorable relationships enhance business outcomes by:

- **Increasing knowledge sharing.** When employees get along and are enthusiastic about their purposes, they are more likely to disclose their best ideas. They are also more likely to look for opportunities to put these ideas into practice. Large social networks increase the likelihood that different perspectives are included in major decisions.

- **Increasing coherence of action.** Successful organizations follow through on their plans. Good ideas are executed in such a way to fully benefit the organizations. On an individual level, higher work capital makes it more likely employees will achieve their professional development goals and are able to maintain healthier lifestyles.

- **Lowering transaction costs.** Mutual trust keeps the lawyers away. Trust also lowers the likelihood of internal disagreements interfering with employee performance. Customers and suppliers can work with a handshake. They will also keep an eye out for improving your work processes and future.

- **Lowering employment costs.** Hiring talent is easier with a reputation of a good place to work. Employees become effective recruiters and are likely to stick around even when work gets challenging. As will be discussed shortly, high social capital reduces the likelihood of accidents, injuries, and illness.

The need for an improved social climate is at the root of many individual and organizational failings. When a hospital president once called me, his first words were, "Judd, we have a popcorn problem." He told me how the nurses like making microwave popcorn and the patients were complaining about the smell—but the nurses were unwilling to stop. This situation made him realize maybe the hospital needed the services of a culture expert. He wisely understood the "popcorn problem" had deeper roots in the organizational culture.

Upon closer examination, it was clear that the nurses and other hospital employees lacked a cohesive culture that inspired cooperation and service. In such a "What's in it for me?" atmosphere, why would anyone give up their popcorn without a fight or at least some compensation? The nurses, it turned out, were not alone in their disgruntlement. The physicians were also at odds, and many were unwilling to refer their patients to anyone working nearby. The situation was so bad that *Money* magazine identified this community as one of the worst places to get sick in America. Fortunately, no one really wanted to work among such unpleasantness. With some assistance and creativity, the members of this work community were able to improve social climate, which made a big difference in quality of medical services and the wellbeing of all concerned.

Rudolf Moos was an early pioneer in conceptualizing the role of social atmosphere in peoples' satisfaction. His interest in identifying core climate factors inspired behavioral scientists and organizational development professionals to explore the role of social atmosphere in a variety of health and productivity outcomes.

In the early 1980s, my father Robert Allen and I did a retrospective study of twenty culture change programs to determine the cultural factors enabling organizations and communities to successfully approach change. This study focused on identifying: (1) factors most significant in blocking solutions to problems prior to the introduction of the change project; and (2) factors that contributed most significantly to the solutions eventually achieved. A subsample of twenty culture change programs (from a list of 616 programs) were selected for inclusion in the study. We concluded that three factors—a sense of community, a shared vision, and a positive outlook—were directly linked to culture change.

- A sense of community exists where there is a high level of trust and openness. People care for one another in times of need. They get to know one another and feel they belong.

- A shared vision exists when an individual recognizes how personal values are actualized through organizational goals. Another important feature of a shared vision is that people recognize their personal values are broadly held. To warrant personal commitment, the vision must be inspirational. A shared vision inspires cooperation and a clear sense of common purpose.

- A positive outlook exists when people call attention to individual and organizational strengths. In an organization with a positive outlook, people know their strengths and build on them. They have the enthusiasm needed to carry out and sustain complex changes. They have some fun together.

Many books and research studies highlight the many benefits of social climate within organizations and communities. In 1999, the Gallup Organization introduced research on employee satisfaction, published in the book, *First Break All the Rules*. In 2000, Robert Putnam published a bestseller, *Bowling Alone*, which shares the tragic health, social and economic implications of declining social climate in American life. In 2016, Charles Vogl published *The Art of Community* featuring many of the techniques used by religious organizations to strengthen the social climate.

Although the evidence in support of social climate is compelling, the tendency exists in individualistic cultures to overlook social climate. We recognize when an individual is positive or optimistic; however, we may overlook the positive or negative nature of the group or organization. We may identify someone as a good team player and friendly, while overlooking cultural qualities associated with a strong sense of community. We are likely to honor visionary leaders, but we may be less aware of how groups and individuals nurture a shared vision.

Assessing Your Team's Social Climate

The following confidential and anonymous survey measures the social climate in your immediate team. You are being asked about the culture among the people with whom you work most closely. Your opinions count even if your answers indicate the culture is not sending clear signals. Your "undecided/don't know" answer also helps when it comes to establishing culture change goals.

Note: There are no incorrect answers. We are asking for your opinion.

Instructions: *Using the five-point scale, rate your level of agreement with the following statements.*

5 strongly agree

4 Agree

3 Neither agree nor disagree / neutral

2 Disagree

1 Strongly disagree

NA Not applicable/don't know

Sense of Community	
I have really gotten to know my coworkers (more than just know what job they do).	5 4 3 2 1 NA
I trust the people I work with.	5 4 3 2 1 NA
I feel comfortable saying what is on my mind.	5 4 3 2 1 NA
I feel like I belong here.	5 4 3 2 1 NA
Coworkers would care for me in a time of need.	5 4 3 2 1 NA
Shared Vision	
I share common values with my coworkers.	5 4 3 2 1 NA
I can explain the mission of the organization.	5 4 3 2 1 NA
I recognize how my own day-to-day activities contribute to the organization's mission.	5 4 3 2 1 NA
I view my team's conduct as consistent with its stated purpose and values.	5 4 3 2 1 NA
I see my team as having a clear and consistent direction.	5 4 3 2 1 NA
I find my work inspiring.	5 4 3 2 1 NA

Positive Outlook	
People in my team have a "can do" attitude.	5 4 3 2 1 NA
I'm proud of the contribution this organization is making.	5 4 3 2 1 NA
Among my immediate coworkers, difficult assignments are treated not as problems, but rather, as special challenges and opportunities.	5 4 3 2 1 NA
My contribution to this organization is recognized.	5 4 3 2 1 NA
I feel optimistic about the future of this organization.	5 4 3 2 1 NA
In my workplace, conflicts are resolved in positive ways.	5 4 3 2 1 NA
In this organization, group or work team achievements are celebrated.	5 4 3 2 1 NA

To determine if you experience a healthy social climate, add all the item scores together and divide by 18 (the number of questions asked). An average above 4 represents a healthy social climate. If your average score is close to 3, addressing your social climate should be a top priority. It will be hard to create a proactive mental health culture if these climate factors are not firmly in place. Most organizations also have plenty of opportunities for improvement. This informative snapshot is a place to begin.

The survey identifies strengths and opportunities for improvement. Consider having your team complete the anonymous Social Climate Survey. The aggregate results reveal eye-opening quantitative information.

The second step in your social climate analysis should be qualitative and should determine factors that led to current results and the best strategies for strengthening the social climate. You are likely to have theories about the current social climate; however, other perspectives add to this information. Informal or more structured interviews can add new insights. Conduct your inquiry in such a way that the interview and sharing of information maintains confidentiality. People don't want to "tell" on their leaders or coworkers. Be sure to include questions about strengths identified by the survey. How did we get those strengths? The interviews should not devolve into a gripe session. The conversation should not end with an overwhelming problem list. The interviews also need to identify solutions. Keep in mind strengths, not weaknesses, help groups move forward. In a strong social climate, teams build on strengths together.

Strengthening the Sense of Community

Organizations enhance their sense of community by building social connection into their policies and procedures. New members can be welcomed and introduced to their coworkers. Face-to-face meetings can include time for "catching up" on personal news. Setting and achieving group goals also helps build community. Post and celebrate special milestones such as marriages, births, and educational achievements.

Organizations should encourage mutual assistance. For

example, the organization could organize buddy systems and peer mentoring. People can be brought together during times of crisis to find ways to help one another.

Community is also nurtured during special occasions. Events such as outdoor adventures and charity functions nurture a sense of community.

In many organizations, distrust undermines the sense of community. Trust can be rebuilt through honest communication, follow-through on commitments, treating people fairly, and by giving people opportunities to get to know and help one another. Trust is a central component of proactive mental health initiatives. Employees need to feel comfortable sharing about their personal goals and struggles. Confidentiality preferences need to be honored. Employers need to be trustworthy by reducing resource barriers and creating supportive conditions for mental health.

One feature of a sense of community is people getting to know each other. When we know each other, we are less likely to stereotype our coworkers. Knowing people in multi-dimensional ways also breaks down prejudices. Many people work together for years without knowing basic things about their coworkers. This can be rectified without people having to share their deepest darkest secrets, so, it is necessary people feel comfortable discussing only those topics that they feel can be shared. Discussing the following topics can deepen community.

- Places you have lived in your life.
- A major change you have made in your life.

- One thing others would need to know with respect to understanding you better.

- A childhood experience that had a lasting effect.

- A person who had a great impact on you.

- How you happened to choose your present work.

- An experience you've had in the last year or two that made a significant impression on you.

- An obstacle you've overcome.

- A personal achievement.

- Your hobbies and special interests.

Story is a vibrant, vital component of community. Stories can communicate what is unique about the history of the group and why people are together. Answers to the following questions can strengthen the sense of community.

- What people, places and purposes brought us together?

- What obstacles have we overcome together?

- How have our products or services made the world a better place?

- How do our current efforts make our futures together brighter?

- What activities, symbols and traditions make us special?

- How do employees make us successful?

Community building need not be an extra activity. It can be built into how work is organized. In some teams:

- New members are introduced to their coworkers.

- There are team goals that can be achieved through collaboration and mutual support.

- Meetings are often face-to-face.

- Meetings include break activities that give people a chance to laugh and play together.

- Social outings are organized for team-building purposes.

- There is an open-door policy that encourages communication.

- Coworkers join in team sports.

- Peer mentoring is organized.

- Opportunities for mutual assistance are embraced.

- Family, housemates, and friends are encouraged to participate in wellness activities and team celebrations.

Varied activities lend themselves to strengthening the sense of community. Too often, these have been seen as "extras." Now, we are learning they are a necessary piece of proactive mental health cultures. Community building just doesn't happen by chance. Leaders can proactively define and advance conditions that strengthen the sense of trust, openness, mutual support, shared history and belonging.

Strengthening the Shared Vision

A shared vision exists when an individual recognizes how personal values are actualized through organizational goals and their personal values are broadly held. To warrant personal commitment, the vision must be inspirational. A shared vision inspires cooperation and a clear sense of common purpose.

How strong is the shared vision in your team? Most teams have strengths and some underdeveloped areas. Hopefully, your organization is not stuck in the past, paralyzed by future projects, or just too busy to strengthen the level of shared vision.

What do plans look like for your team? Does it look like a wish list or simply a repetition of last year's goals? Goals don't have to be hard to achieve to be inspirational. However, they should be grounded in the dreams and aspirations of all involved. They should represent a common cause.

Following-through with a plan is essential to a successful shared vision. In many organizations, goals feel unstable when there are no objectives, timelines, or delegation of responsibilities.

Organizational policies and practices need to be aligned with the vision. Ask employees about policy changes that would demonstrate commitment to the vision. Are the right things being rewarded? Is the communication compelling and consistent? Are leaders good role models? Are our traditions consistent with our vision? Are people taught the skills needed to achieve the vision? Is the onboarding process for new employees getting people on the right track?

Are resources such as time, space, and money allocated consistent with the vision?

"Organizations and teams must respond to changing job demands, new technologies, and broader societal changes. Constant change can undermine the sense of share vision, particularly if there is little follow-through on prior decisions and goals. Following-through with a plan is essential to a successful shared vision. In many organizations, goals feel unstable when there are no objectives, timelines, or delegation of responsibilities. When new goals are introduced, plans for aligning the culture and support systems should be a part of the conversation. Frustration occurs when good ideas do not get realized because of lack of follow-through. Many shared vision goals require a year or years to achieve. A strong shared vision tends to require an action plan beginning with a proper analysis, introduction, integration, and evaluation.

Chapter 8 of *We Flourish* features this four-phase process for changing the proactive mental health culture. Such a step-by-step approach to change strengthens the shared vision.

Shared visions are enlivened and energized by a narrative that rings true. Many visions build on the dreams and vision of the organization's founders, even if the founder is long gone. For example, a shared vision for The Walt Disney Company would probably resonate if it matched Walt's creative vision. Similarly, a shared vision for Johnson & Johnson would be strengthened if based on its founding credo. The future can break from the past if such a transition has a compelling and unifying reason. For example, a college known as a party school could build a divergent vision after a series of alcohol-related deaths. Develop your cultural story and narrative to strengthen your vision of a healthy and productive culture.

Each organization and team is unique. The shared stories, traditions, heroes, norms, and innovations make people feel special and support a shared vision.

- What symbols, rituals, and rites will be our own?
- Who will be the heroes and role models?
- What special cultural norms will we maintain?
- How will our organization's—or team's—story be different?

With a shared vision, people see their personal values reflected in how work gets done and how the organization operates. Sometimes this idea is stated in core values or principles to help people connect their values to the organization. A shared vision incorporates shared values. In a broader culture often calling attention to differences, it is easy to overlook the importance of shared values. A great exercise for determining shared values could start with these three steps:

1. Have coworkers share personal values significant to their work. Then check the level of agreement that each person's values are worthwhile.

2. Review values meaningful to the organization's founders or part of the origin story.

3. Identify four or five core values that both encompass individual values and reflect the values held by the organization's founders.

Each organization boasts benefits, such as the opportunity to make a great product or offer a very helpful service. Some jobs test peoples' skills and give them an opportunity to learn new skills. Some jobs provide insurance and some financial security in retirement. A full value proposition (understanding these many organizational benefits) is meaningful to a shared vision, as people respond to different benefits.

Proactive mental health needs to become part of the shared vision and work value proposition.

Just as jobs offer value to the work, efforts to promote proactive mental health can also deliver a variety of benefits. Many employers have focused exclusively on the cost savings from reducing mental illness. While an important benefit, proactive mental health delivers more than cost savings on medical care and absenteeism. Some people, especially employees not motivated by cost-savings, will like the other quality-of-life benefits. A CEO might, for example, like proactive mental health because it reduces mental illness and saves money. A coworker might say he likes proactive mental health because it makes him more productive both at work and in his family responsibilities. A shared vision for proactive mental health does not require everyone adopt the same favorite outcomes. They are all a part of the package.

Strengthening the Positive Outlook

A negative culture stifles initiative, exacerbates disagreements, and saps energy. Unfortunately, the broader culture tends to be negative. In school we are taught to focus on what is wrong. The news focuses on tragic stories and improper behavior.

In order to form a positive culture, we must recognize our strengths, not our weaknesses, enable us to move forward. A strength review is a powerful tool. Try to organize a deep analysis of existing capabilities before addressing new challenges.

Language is important in a positive culture. In a positive culture, you are less likely to hear people call things problems. You are more likely to hear people expressing similar ideas using the words challenges and opportunities. You are also more likely to hear the word "and" than the word "but." Without the "but," you are less likely to discount meaningful ideas or actions.

The language we use and the ways we categorize our information play important roles in establishing a positive culture. As a case in point, mental health programs have sometimes focused on language that fall into the negative framework.

- Will we focus on surviving or thriving?

- Will we focus on mental illness or mental health?

- Will we focus on blame and guilt or on getting results?

- Will we focus on past mistakes or future opportunities?

- Will we focus on personal weakness or personal strengths?

- Will we focus on dependencies or being connected?

As can be seen in these examples, we could adjust the messages and practice of proactive mental health initiatives, so they are more affirming and positive.

Programs addressing mental health are too often undermined by negative language and cultures. The focus had been on managing mental illness and addressing crisis. A more positive approach would also focus on mental health strengths, fun, mutual support, and kindness that would also empower individuals to adopt proactive mental health behaviors and attitudes. By adopting such a positive framework, we are less likely to see people as disabled and victims. We are more likely to recognize each person's potential.

Professor Martin Seligman of the Positive Psychology Center at University of Pennsylvania is probably best known for his studies of rats escaping electric shocks. Those rats that could control when they received a shock were healthier than rats that were simply shocked at the same time. Dr. Seligman called this lack of control *learned helplessness*. This study is a reminder to all of us that we want to give people as much control over their work and struggles as possible.

More recently, Dr. Seligman created a positive psychology framework for thinking about an individual's pessimism and optimism that could also be applied to the goal of creating positive cultures. Just as individuals can uphold negative or positive attitudes, cultures can be optimistic. In such a positive culture, it is a norm to view: (1) setbacks as temporary rather than permanent, (2) criticism as constructive and not personal, and (3) negative situations as limited in scope rather than pervasive. These lessons of positive psychology can become cultural norms.

In a positive culture, we learn from experience. A bad outcome is not as overwhelming if it leads to new and improved strategies. This mindset is part of grit, or an individual's perseverance of effort combined with the passion for a particular long-term goal or end state. This continuous learning or idea iteration improve outcomes by integrating new information and modifying unsuccessful approaches.

In a negative culture, two satisfying outcomes are too often viewed as win-lose tradeoffs. Win-win opportunities tend to be overlooked. These win-lose cultural traps are called false dichotomies. These occur when two positive outcomes are viewed as tradeoffs even when success with one would increase the likelihood of success with the other. Most teams have false dichotomies that undermine a positive outlook. The win-win approach needs to supplant these energy-draining tradeoffs. A classic false dichotomy in business views the goals of management as competing with the goals of workers. The win-win is preferable. If workers succeed, they are going to be more engaged. If managers succeed, workers are going to get more autonomy and potentially more compensation. A classic mental health example is the mistaken tradeoff between a goal for treating illness versus a goal for healthy living. There is a win-win. When we get sick, mental health professionals need to recommend proactive mental health behaviors. Lifestyle change skills and supportive environments come in handy to the treatment recommendations. Those enthusiastic about proactive mental health know it's challenging adopting better personal practices when you are mentally ill. Both treatment and prevention are paramount to favorable health outcomes.

Some television comedies such as *Saturday Night Live* got their start making fun of people with mannerisms that set them apart. In a negative culture, fun and funny tend to be at someone's expense, leading some organizations to try to discourage joking. We don't have to dull down and dampen our senses of humor. We can play, laugh, and love with much less ridicule.

In a positive culture, successes are celebrated. In a negative culture, celebrations are rare. Recognizing success is derided as unnecessary or bragging. Such criticism can be overcome by celebrating group successes and by finding intermediate goals to celebrate. When we celebrate small achievements, we can build courage and resiliency for celebrating our larger goals.

Achieving Proactive Mental Health and Social Climate

Organizational innovation, customer satisfaction, teamwork and employee well-being depend on an uplifting work atmosphere. Social climate should be considered whenever new human resource policies and procedures are introduced. We must ask, for example, do these new actions build community, foster a shared vision, and engender a positive outlook? We can organize policies and procedures such as training, rewards, modeling, traditions, and communication in such a way that they enhance and do not undermine social climate. In this rapidly changing world, our actions should not undermine social networks, trust, and openness. We should look for ways to strengthen interpersonal relationships, to co-create solutions, and to enjoy collaboration.

When we strengthen social climate, we will increase our likelihood of personal well-being and organizational growth. Perhaps most importantly, by enhancing social climate we will be less likely to view social influences as impediments to individual freedom and progress. Instead, we will be more likely to experience the positive role of social bonds in health, happiness, innovation, and productivity.

Chapter 6

Strengthen Proactive Mental Health Norms

"For to change the norms, the very foci of attention, of a cultural system is a difficult task—far more complex than that of changing an individual's attitudes and interests."

—JAMES S. COLEMAN

CULTURAL NORMS ARE social expectations regarding attitudes and behavior. It is "the way we do things around here." A common example is the informal expectation for whether and how much to tip for service. Another example is related to driving motor vehicles. In many parts of the United States, it is a norm to drive at least five miles above the posted speed limit. Getting a traffic ticket for driving at that speed would be considered unreasonable by many.

Norms play a significant role in promoting or undermining

proactive mental health. It's difficult to function without social norms. Sociologist Émile Durkheim found that a lack of social norms can lead to suicide. Loneliness and normlessness are primary factors in anxiety, depression, and other forms of mental illness. Many employees experienced this sense of normlessness when they were asked to work at home. No clear norms were evident regarding how to collaborate, when to work, or how to balance work and home life. New norms were needed to accommodate the stay-at-home worker.

Rarely are norms written into policies or laws. Instead, they tend to operate on a subconscious level. Leaders work with their teams and mental health experts to identify key norms that need strengthening or changing. For example, an initiative to improve sleep focused on establishing a norm for sleeping between seven and eight hours daily and a norm for napping during some work breaks. These norm goals were based on workplace concerns about how inadequate sleep causes health consequences and safety challenges.

In Chapter 2, attitudes and behaviors are identified as proactive mental health priorities. All six proactive mental health building blocks would be easier to achieve if those attitudes and behaviors were also norms. It is helpful to gather employee input on some of the most common proactive mental health goals. The Proactive Mental Health Cultural Norm Indicator can assess the existing culture and help set norm change goals.

Proactive Mental Health Team Norms Survey

Organizational culture is crucial to supporting mental health. Our behavior is influenced by the groups to which we belong. Our family, friends, and coworkers are examples of these groups; they all have expectations for how people should behave, even when it comes to mental health practices.

The following confidential and anonymous survey measures how this works in your immediate team, those people with whom you have the most contact. Survey results will be used to help enhance initiatives to prevent mental illness.

Note: There are no wrong answers. We are asking for your opinion.

There may be some statements not applicable to you, if, for example, you have almost no contact with co-workers. For such statements select NA for not applicable.

Instructions: *Please indicate your level of agreement with the statements using the following scale:*

5 Strongly Agree
4 Agree
3 Undecided/Don't Know
2 Disagree
1 Strongly Disagree
NA Not Applicable

It is accepted and expected among my immediate co-workers to...

Come to work rested.	5 4 3 2 1 NA
Take on only as much responsibility as can be handled.	5 4 3 2 1 NA
Practice some form of stress management technique.	5 4 3 2 1 NA
Achieve a balance between work, rest, and play.	5 4 3 2 1 NA
Organize work to avoid injury (such as office layout, lighting, lifting and safety gear).	5 4 3 2 1 NA
Eat nutritious foods that are low in salt, fat and sugar.	5 4 3 2 1 NA
Exercise at least most days.	5 4 3 2 1 NA
Drink alcohol moderately, if at all.	5 4 3 2 1 NA
Take only those drugs that are medically necessary.	5 4 3 2 1 NA
Get help with mental health, alcohol, or other drug problems early on.	5 4 3 2 1 NA
Stay current on health screenings and preventative medicine.	5 4 3 2 1 NA
Find ways to make every day or routine tasks interesting.	5 4 3 2 1 NA
Find times to kick back and relax.	5 4 3 2 1 NA
Develop work and career skills.	5 4 3 2 1 NA
Achieve financial security.	5 4 3 2 1 NA
Be open to new ideas and experiences.	5 4 3 2 1 NA

It is accepted and expected among my immediate co-workers to...

Explore talents and interests.	5 4 3 2 1 NA
Be persistent and follow through on goals.	5 4 3 2 1 NA
Develop a sense of spirituality or meaning in life.	5 4 3 2 1 NA
Be honest and rarely withhold information.	5 4 3 2 1 NA
Find ways to renew and develop friendships.	5 4 3 2 1 NA
Say hello.	5 4 3 2 1 NA
Share credit for success.	5 4 3 2 1 NA
Treat all people with respect regardless of sex, age, race, disability, or sexual preference.	5 4 3 2 1 NA
Appreciate the value of having a variety of backgrounds and traditions.	5 4 3 2 1 NA
Be a good listener.	5 4 3 2 1 NA
Respond in times of need.	5 4 3 2 1 NA
Ask for help when it is needed.	5 4 3 2 1 NA
Join a support group when faced with a continuing health problem (such as cancer).	5 4 3 2 1 NA
Celebrate accomplishments.	5 4 3 2 1 NA
Resolve conflict in positive ways.	5 4 3 2 1 NA
Treat people fairly in terms of pay and other rewards.	5 4 3 2 1 NA

Hopefully, your workgroup's norms embody many existing strengths to build upon. Most workgroups would benefit from establishing several proactive mental health norms that exploit behaviors and attitudes to mirror.

There are 32 questions. An average score can be determined by adding all the item scores together and dividing by 32. An average above 4 represents a strong proactive mental health culture. If your average score is close to 3, your culture is not sending clear signals supporting proactive mental health. A strong culture with firm norms for behavior feels restrictive and lacking in spontaneity. A weak culture without clear cultural norms tends to be disorienting. In such cultures, it is tough to coordinate effective teamwork. Most organizations have plenty of opportunities for improvement. This enlightening snapshot is a place to begin.

Changing norms will require considerable focus. Starting with two or three closely aligned norm goals (for example, those regarding getting adequate sleep) are usually sufficient. Fortunately, new norm goals can be set once the current norm goals are achieved. Organizations and teams have evolving proactive mental health priorities. For example, the disruptive impact of accelerated communication technology is a hot topic in many organizations. Many employees are struggling how to balance twenty-hour communication with an appropriate balance between work, rest, and play. In such settings, establishing norms for how and when to respond to business-related requests would be a priority. In other organizations, norms that would reduce sexual discrimination and harassment would be the priority right now. Setting goals for normative change is ongoing. Previously unforeseen goals are likely to emerge as work demands evolve, broader societal conditions change, and new technologies are adopted.

Change Norms by Realigning Cultural Touchpoints

Leaders at all levels can co-create new norms by working with their teams to align day-to-day cultural influences called cultural touchpoints. Cultural touchpoints are formal and informal policies and practices. These social factors are called touchpoints in that they represent day-to-day influences on behavior. An example would be policies prohibiting sexual harassment. However, the most common touchpoints are usually experienced through informal mechanisms. Many of these informal mechanism work against stated policy and proactive mental health. An illustration of this would be the all-too-common office practice of rewarding and recognizing those who work through lunch. It is often necessary to modify several touchpoints to establish new proactive mental health norms. So, for example, a desired norm for getting adequate sleep would best be established through a combination of providing information about recommended sleep practices, assisting with soundproofing employees' bedrooms, pushing back against coming to work when tired, and providing designated places for napping. There are fourteen primary touchpoints.

Primary Cultural Touchpoints

1. Resource Commitment
2. Built Environment
3. Communication and Information
4. Rewards and Recognition
5. Relationship Development (Make it Social)
6. Learning and Training
7. Modeling
8. Pushback
9. Onboarding
10. Traditions and Symbols
11. Story and Narrative
12. Roles and Responsibilities
13. Goal Setting and Planning
14. Laws and Policies

1. Resource Commitment Touchpoint

The resource commitment touchpoint includes how time, money and other resources are allocated. Having a budget for a proactive mental health makes it possible to hire professionals, improve communication, modify the physical environment, and fund healthful activities. Such a budget makes both a symbolic statement about the importance of proactive mental health and reduces barriers. Resources also must be considered in how work practices and work schedules are determined. In a proactive mental health culture, decisions about such resources reflect consideration for the mental health of employees.

In a proactive mental health culture, there are adequate resources to carry out mental health-related recommendations. Trial runs and a gradual roll-out of proactive mental health initiatives can identify barriers. When obvious barriers such as schedule conflicts, logistical barriers, and malfunctioning technology are not addressed, confidence is undermined. A recent experience at a university helps to illustrate this point. Department chairs were told to offer healthy choices during meetings. Unfortunately, none of the approved vendors offered such healthy choices. As a result, the department chairs lost confidence in the university's health initiative.

Employees have cultural beliefs about resource shortfalls. Ask employees to describe the resources that would show the organization's commitment to proactive mental health. In one company, the most common request was to provide adequate and well-lit employee parking. In another organization, those working on the factory floor requested a convenient water fountain.

2. Built Environment Touchpoint

Proactive mental health should be taken into consideration when choosing and designing workspaces. The built environment includes decisions about where people work, how buildings are laid out, individual workspace design, and even the grounds surrounding the workplace. Employees, at all levels, should and inevitably will have valuable input about creating uplifting environments that nurture both mental health and productivity.

Employees can help identify current strengths and ways the physical environment could better support their mental health. In one organization, the lack of parking and the resulting competition for parking space was a daily stressor. In another Florida-based organization, employee noted the lack of showers made it difficult to exercise during work breaks.

Work environments need to be conducive to both productivity and personal well-being. On a hot factory floor, cool drinking water made work both unpleasant and unhealthy. When employees were introduced to relaxation techniques, a quiet place to practice them was needed. The layout, lighting, ventilation, noise, flow, and usability of buildings and grounds play important roles in mental health. Is the space well-maintained, uncluttered, and up to date? Is there access to natural light? Are buildings designed compatibly with surrounding architecture?

Employers can locate their workplaces with mental health in mind. Can employees find affordable, safe, and desirable housing nearby? Do people feel safe getting to and leaving from work? Are there local proactive mental health amenities such as parks, indoor fitness facilities, and nearby healthy eating establishments? Is convenient and affordable child-care available? Are there sufficient parking and efficient public transportation options? If people are working from home, are households large enough and otherwise suitable for work?

The design of workspaces, common spaces, and how people circulate through buildings impact social connections. Where possible, employees should have spaces to greet and intermingle. Computers and automation may cut the number of workers and reduce the likelihood of positive social interaction. What used to be a social job may now be one done in isolation. Find ways to mitigate this loss of social connection.

Where possible, employees should be empowered to help tailor their workplace to their preferences. Personal touches such as plants, photos, art, lighting, and color schemes can be tangible elements of psychological well-being.

3. Communication Touchpoint

Misinformation about mental health needs to be addressed. Employees may, for example, falsely assume few people experience mental illness. The unspoken message suggests we should be embarrassed or avoid getting help. Many people hide their troubles. Lack of communication and lack of transparency have been counterproductive.

Proactive mental health is a diverse topic encompassing safety, social connections, presence, purpose, health behavior, and adaptability. The science and recommendations are continuously being updated. Employees need to be kept abreast of the best ways to maintain good mental health and of mental health resources available at work and in the community. They also need information about how they can support the mental health of co-workers, friends, and family. In a proactive mental health culture, employees:

- Stay current on topics related to proactive mental health.

- Obtain proactive mental health messages that resonate. The culture must be considered to establish effective communication. In some cultures, person-to-person communication is most effective. In other cultures, communication must come from a particular person to be valued. Communication is often determined by language proficiency, education and even access to technology.

- Draw clear and updated information about what the proactive mental health initiative is, why it's important, and how people can participate.

- Share information about the best workplace and community resources for proactive mental health.

- Gain regular feedback on how they are doing individually and at an aggregate team level.

- Feel their preferences regarding confidentiality are honored.

- Feel comfortable sharing their proactive mental health goals and needs.

- Let coworkers know of their willingness to support them.

4. Rewards and Recognition Touchpoint

Most workplaces have both formal and informal systems of rewards and recognition. Salary is an example of the formal reward system. Early access to information, special job assignments, flexible work schedules, and praise are examples of informal rewards. The goal with the rewards and recognition touchpoint is to encourage a broad range of proactive mental health attitudes and behavior and to stop rewarding unhealthy attitudes and behavior.

Culture sets the standard for how rewards are perceived. A valued reward in one culture would be disparaged as a bribe or insult in another culture. Groups accustomed to incentives tend to value cash rewards. Professional groups tend to value praise from colleagues. Those facing long commutes are likely to value permission to work from home. The greatest impact is achieved by tailoring rewards to individual needs and subcultures, as one size does not fit all. Many organizations make this mistake by relying exclusively on financial rewards.

Unhealthy practices are sometimes established and maintained by rewards. For example, employees are commonly and mistakenly rewarded for coming to work sick or for sacrificing work breaks and vacations. Using unhealthy baked goods and sweets as rewards is another common mistake. Reducing rewards for unhealthy practices and reducing unhealthy rewards are important proactive mental health strategies. Ideally, the nature of the reward will reinforce proactive mental health, such as a coupon good for the purchase of fitness-related shoes sends a clearer message than other rewards would.

Offer a mix of individual and group rewards. Some proactive mental health programs incentivize individual behavior like completing health behavior assessments and watching informational videos. A larger impact could be achieved by including team rewards. Peer support, team spirit and encouragement would be activated through such group rewards.

Using rewards is tricky, as they often have unintended and undesirable consequences.

- The quickest way to stop a behavior is to pay someone to do something and then stop paying them.

- Material rewards can distract employees from intrinsic rewards such as the health benefits of positive practices.

- Rewards are often seen as unjust, particularly true when rewards are tied in with health insurance costs. Such incentives can feel like a way for employers to reduce their commitment to paying for health insurance. Concerns arise around setting up a system where people might be inclined to cheat, thereby increasing the level of distrust at work. Some employers show their distrust by requiring doctors and others to verify information.

5. Relationships Touchpoint

People are social animals and inclined towards activities that build and invigorate relationships. One proactive mental health strategy would increase the opportunities to meet people through healthy activities. Another strategy is to reduce the likelihood that unhealthy practices, such as overeating or excess drinking, will be primary social opportunities. Include existing social networks with family and friends in the proactive mental health initiative. Promote use of community resources such as fitness clubs and parks. Our need for social connections should help and not undermine proactive mental health.

Cultures establish how relationships are formed and maintained. In some organizations, people are unlikely to form friendships at work; in others, there are few opportunities for leaders to interact with lower-level employees. While still other organizations have strong norms for leadership by walking around and collaborating in common areas; in such cultures, there are fewer formal rules for how people connect.

In a proactive mental health culture, healthy activities, and conversations present opportunities for people to get to know one another. Informal social networks enhance mental health. One culture strategy is to replace unhealthy social groups with healthier alternatives. Gatherings at designated smoking areas, vending machines, fast food restaurants and bar rooms should no longer be the best social opportunities. In contrast, fitness activities, healthier restaurants and arts happenings could become the social hot spots.

Another culture strategy is to invite family and friends to participate in proactive mental health activities. At a minimum, educational programs could be extended to employees' social networks. Such an approach mobilizes the natural support network and fosters proactive mental health norms at home.

Community engagement is another relationship development strategy with the goal to connect employees with healthy social activities available in the community. Employers can also co-sponsor community efforts to promote the six building blocks of proactive mental health.

6. Learning and Training Touchpoint

People are more likely to adopt behaviors they excel in. Increasing training for healthy behavior and reducing learning and training supporting unhealthy practices would help support a proactive mental health culture. For better and for worse, culture greatly influences how and what people learn. Informal training offered by coworkers is often more frequent and comprehensive than online, classroom, and mentoring programs. Many people learn unhealthy behavior through their peers. For example, night shift workers and those working in the transportation industry often share methods for going without sleep. Most smokers and drug abusers learned about their habits from peers. One culture strategy is to help employees bond with more health-minded peer groups.

Some proactive mental health initiatives have a training component. One culture strategy is to make sure the training is in line with organizational policies. So, for example, the duration and location of training should match up with employee schedules. Accommodate diverse learning preferences and abilities and offer employees a choice by including online delivery, in printed form, and in meeting rooms. Language and educational differences should be considered. Training offerings should be available to those working offsite or in the evening. Consider recording and sharing trainings so that they are available to employees' social network. Employees will find it easier to achieve new behaviors if family and friends also have needed skills.

7. Modeling Touchpoint

People learn from watching others. Through role models, employees witness the impact and desirability of attitudes and behavior. The modeling touchpoint elevates the visibility of coworkers and leaders practicing proactive mental health, while reducing the visibility and negative impact of those modeling unhealthy practices. An example of a negative role model would be an executive who brags about working all the time. Ideally, there would be good role models for each of the six proactive mental health building blocks (i.e., presence, adaptability, connection, safety, health behavior, and purpose).

Cultures differ in who is seen as role models. Role models distinguish themselves through a variety of qualifications including being a long-time employee, achieving the highest rank, and being the most capable in solving work challenges. In a proactive mental health culture, role models share their mental health success stories. Role models demonstrate what is possible with a variety of proactive mental health goals.

Sometimes role models are needed to make a new practice acceptable. At one corporate headquarters, few people used the walking path. Employees said using the path would suggest their workloads were too light. This all changed when the entire legal department, known to be the hardest working, took daily walks. Soon after, many teams were walking the path.

One culture change strategy is to assist role models to visibly engage in proactive mental health. Role models can demonstrate a personal commitment by enthusiastically participating in proactive mental health activities, by adopting a healthy lifestyle, and by making their healthy practices more visible.

A second culture strategy would be to reduce the impact of those role models not currently committed to personal or organizational proactive mental health. This could be as simple as asking those role models to reduce the visibility of their unhealthy practices.

A third culture strategy is to create new role models. The heroic stories of employees' personal achievements would be widely publicized and shared. Employees would be honored for their special efforts to help others. Ideally, there would be an abundance of role models available from diverse backgrounds and diverse achievements.

8. Pushback Touchpoint

There are many forms of pushback. Other words for pushback are *confrontation, boundaries, penalties,* and *consequences.* Sometimes pushback is spelled out in a policy manual of *do's* and *don'ts.* No-smoking policies and their consequences are examples of pushback. Sexual abuse policies and their consequences are a relatively recent addition to using the pushback touchpoint. On the flip side, it is all too common for healthy behavior to be confronted. Someone trying a new healthy practice might be ridiculed as a "health nut." The goal is to reduce pushback against healthy and productive behavior and to increase pushback against unhealthy practices.

Some workplaces are viewed as having too many rules. Such workplaces are perceived to be cruel, unjust, and oppressive. When pushback is working well, it is perceived as helpful guidance in the spirit of public good.

Pushback can play a positive role in a proactive mental health culture. The pushback touchpoint includes actions such as enforcing sexual harassment policies and reducing pushback against healthy activities. An example of this would be to encourage—rather than discourage—employees sticking with clear boundaries for reduced communication during non-work hours.

Engage employees in decisions about pushback. Employees voted on a policy not to leave sweets in the break room. This was pushback against those generously leaving baked goods for others. After the vote, it was easier for all to agree on limiting such treats to Fridays. When employees co-create pushback policies, there is better buy-in and a greater feeling of empowerment and ownership for the successful outcomes.

When introducing a new restriction and consequence, provide sufficient warning and support for personal change. This lesson was learned the hard way when no smoking policies were first introduced. Many smokers did not get the support they needed to quit in advance of the policy. The policy was not sufficiently introduced as a public health measure for all employees. These missteps created an atmosphere of bitterness and distrust.

Go lightly with pushback. Policies and laws are powerful proactive mental health strategies. They have a track record of addressing everything from safety issues at work to promoting the forty-hour work week. However, this strategy goes against important proactive mental health values of personal choice and freedom. Pushback is a solution of last resort. It can be phased in after implementing a broader array of culture change strategies.

9. Onboarding Touchpoint

Onboarding, also known as *recruitment, selection, welcome,* and *orientation*, refers to the process by which new employees acquire the necessary knowledge, skills, and behaviors necessary to become effective organizational members and insiders. Onboarding is the organizational equivalent of acculturation, including both the formal and informal aspects of recruitment, selection, and orientation.

One culture change strategy is to modify the informal and formal onboarding process to no longer run counter to proactive mental health. Old hazing experiences involving excessive work expectations would be replaced by a less jarring workload. A prior sink-or-swim approach to social connections would be replaced by friendly introductions and mentoring.

The organization should encourage a reputation as happy, healthy, and supportive place to work. One goal is to highlight the proactive mental health initiative in recruitment messages.

The goal of selection is to pick candidates who are open and enthusiastic about opportunities for proactive mental health. A strong candidate is likely to support others. In a proactive mental health culture, the selection process gives candidates opportunities to express their openness to perusing personal proactive mental health. Preference is given to those candidates who show an interest in proactive mental health.

In a proactive mental health culture, new employees are informed about the vision and purpose of the proactive mental health program. This is both a part of the formal orientation process and a part of early on-the-job experiences. Where a supportive culture is in place, new employees are likely to form early and potentially deep workplace friendships around healthy activities.

The first days and weeks on the new job should spring people into this exciting part of their identity and sense of responsibility by not undermining mental health behavior. These early job experiences should be welcoming and make it possible for new employees to settle into healthy tasks and routines. New employees should be given an opportunity to share their early impressions. Is proactive mental health being fully supported? Where are the gaps? Do they have suggestions based on prior employment experiences?

10. Traditions and Symbols Touchpoint

When cultures assign meaning to repeated actions and events, they become traditions and symbols. Annual holiday parties, summer picnics, and annual reports are examples of organizational traditions. A morning greeting and coffee break are examples of daily traditions. Some work groups celebrate birthdays, the birth of children, and retirement.

Some traditions may be modified or eliminated. In one ski area, for example, it was a tradition for lift operators to party daily and go without sleep. This tradition resulted in increased burnout by the month of March. This matched reduced staffing needs for the spring skiing season, but the tradition was not compatible with proactive mental health. In a similar way, some traditions were created during an era when sexism and racism was somewhat accepted. These traditions need to be updated/upgraded for proactive mental health.

Most traditions provide important proactive mental health functions. They bolster the sense of community and foster a more positive outlook. It can be beneficial to revitalize traditions, even if the activities are not that healthy.

One goal with existing traditions and symbols is to add a healthful element or at least give people healthy options. Providing healthy food choices would be an example a proactive mental health change. Including proactive mental health goals in the annual report could be a symbol that the initiative is lauded.

Many organizations have abandoned their traditions and symbols. Birthdays, holidays, and anniversaries used to be celebrated. Fill the void with new traditions and symbols to establish proactive mental health. Some meetings, for example, could include times for standing and for stretching. Your organization could adopt a community fitness event such as a fun run or charity challenge. Employees could support the event from the sidelines. Other employees could join in the activity. A team may want to establish a new mental health tradition such as annual participation in symposium on a mental health challenge in the news.

11. Story and Narrative Touchpoint

Culture can be expressed in a plot with key characters, heroes, villains, chapters, morals, victories, and defeats. For example, most organizational cultures embrace a story about their founding, purpose, and future. Such stories are frequently based on qualities of the organization's founders and can have a profound impact on what is acceptable and worthy within the culture.

The goal with the story and narrative touchpoint is to include proactive mental health in the story about the founding purpose and future of the organization. The way the story is told should emphasize the value of people. The dimensions of proactive mental health can be recognized in this story.

The role of employees is central and the story of how the culture committed to promoting mental health is the plot. At a railroad, for example, the narrative began with a concern for safety. The trains were crashing at tremendous cost of life and property. It evolved to understanding the work required being well-rested, free of substance abuse, and a heightened commitment to safety.

The narrative should incorporate a culturally appropriate list of proactive mental health benefits. In one organization, the CEO mistakenly reduced proactive mental health to a strategy for controlling the costs associated with absenteeism. In this culture, the CEO's story sounded greedy. Employees resisted proactive mental health. They viewed the program as a violation of personal freedoms. A more compelling story could have identified a win-win wherein lives could be saved as well as money.

Teams and subculture should be encouraged to add their special chapter in the overall proactive mental health story. This chapter should include personal victories and heroic efforts to support others. The story should include roles for proactive mental health champions and other leaders who addressed barriers. There should also be stories of how the team achieved healthful actions together.

12. Roles and Responsibilities Touchpoint

There are several important roles and responsibilities in any culture-change process. Human resource professionals often have corresponding knowledge and experience needed to address barriers and increase support. Champions are needed within senior leadership, middle management and within work groups. Mental health professionals, such as counselors and therapists, also need to support the initiative.

Employees have personal responsibilities to incorporate proactive mental health into their lives and goals and to offer peer support.

Proactive mental health calls for powerful and persuasive champions. In some cultures, leading proactive mental health will be the responsibility of the CEO or human resources director. Larger organizations tend to assign this responsibility to those providing employee assistance programs and the chief medical officer. In smaller organizations, proactive mental health leadership might be exclusively the responsibility of middle-managers.

Subject matter experts also stimulate and help to sustain proactive mental health. Nutritionists, personal trainers, yoga instructors, health coaches are examples of proactive mental health experts. Each brings pertinent knowledge and guidance into the culture, which can be a game changer (or outright victory). The culture determines the extent to which such resource people can assist employees.

Middle managers play important leadership roles in establishing a proactive mental health culture within their teams. They should receive leadership training, as well as a budget and/or decision-making authority. At a minimum, these leaders need to communicate with senior management about what is happening within their team.

Employees should have clear proactive mental health responsibilities. In a proactive mental health culture, there is an expectation employees will pursue at least one personal goal annually. Additional responsibilities include providing peer support to coworkers, family, and housemates.

13.Goal Setting and Planning Touchpoint

Most cultures have established ways to plan and carry out change. Proactive mental health goals should become part of the strategic plan or built into the annual assessments and whatever dashboard is used to track progress.

Proactive mental health should be included in workplace goals and plans for achieving them. Each culture establishes norms for goal setting and planning. Some of these will be organization-wide others are set at the team level. Employees can also be encouraged to include personal proactive mental health goals in their annual plans. There are a variety of goals and plans in most workplaces: an annual strategic plan; a formal budgeting approval process; an authorization process to approve plans before time and other resources can be allocated; employees have an annual review process working with their immediate supervisors to set work goals. Each of these examples provide an opportunity to include proactive mental health goals for every layer of an organization.

When goals are being established, proactive mental health should be included in both short-term goals and the long-term strategic plan. This could be as simple as asking about the impact of a decision on mental health. In groups driven by goals and plans, the proactive mental health initiative could create psychological space for spontaneity and fun. Offering this balance could be a much-appreciated part of the plan. The proactive mental health initiative could focus on bringing some order and follow-through to the work culture. In organizations that tend not to follow through on goals, the proactive mental health initiative could set a new higher standard for being organized around achieving goals. Proactive mental health initiatives could model a more organized approach. For example, seminars on mindfulness could be followed by a plan for ongoing support participants. The initiative would track and celebrate progress.

Many organizations neglect goal setting at the team level. Health assessments and program participation data are aggregated for the entire organization. When this happens, the team has no way to know how it is doing. In such organizations, the lack of goals and subsequent planning undermines the credibility and efficacy of the program. In a proactive mental health culture, teams fix goals in place and make plans specific to the nature of the work. For instance, employees who work at desks may benefit from support for stretch breaks. Employees who work night shifts might set goals for supporting healthy sleep. Setting such team-level goals and plans enhances the proactive mental health culture.

14. Laws and Policies Touchpoint

Laws and policies can have a significant influence on personal behavior. Examples of laws influencing proactive mental health include requiring the use of car safety belts and prohibiting smoking indoors. Organizations also often have policies regarding appropriate work behavior. Many of these rules became less relevant when employees began to work from home.

Policies and laws tend to be very effective, but they can feel oppressive. People value free choice. Some organizations author and enforce a thick policy manual with many rules governing employee conduct. Less formal organizations rely primarily on local laws to govern workplace behavior.

Having something in the policy manual does not always make it a norm. In some cultures, there is strict adherence to policy and laws, while in other teams, policies and laws are merely treated as "suggestions." Norms often take over the rulemaking. Some norms may contradict both policies and laws. Such would be the case in the trucking industry, where often the norm is to drive over the speed limit.

Do an inventory of your workplace policies to see how they support or undermine employee mental health. Consider safety policies. Some organizations have rules requiring specified daily work breaks and vacations. Sometimes you may find it necessary to advocate for changes in workplace policies. For example, young employees with children lack policies supporting parental leave or policies accommodating child-care and school schedules. A policy could be written that better accommodates the family responsibilities. For example, a shift in work hours could reduce the commute times.

Some supportive policies are not norms. In many teams, for example, employees commonly work through lunch, even when the policy calls for a lunch break. When good policies and laws go unheeded, your focus should be on raising awareness and removing barriers to healthy behavior. The goal is to establish norms consistent with the positive policies and laws. Use positive reinforcement and avoid penalties whenever possible.

On rare occasions, policies undermine or contradict proactive mental health initiatives. For example, a company could authorize purchases from vendors that only sell unhealthy foods. Another common example involves a lack of flexibility in work schedules. Changes would be required for employees to attend proactive mental health programs.

Aligning Cultural Touchpoints with Culture Change Goals

Cultures are webs of influences on attitudes and behavior. Each cultural touchpoint plays a role in day-to-day cultural influences and in establishing cultural norms. Answers to the following questions are useful for planning how to better align touchpoints with cultural support for proactive mental health:

- **RESOURCE COMMITMENT:** Do people have the time and tools and equipment they need to behave in a way that is consistent with culture-change goals? Does the allocation of resources send the mistaken message that desirable behavior is not important? Who will lead changes in the allocation of resources (e.g., money, time, information)? What support will be needed to propel such changes?

- **BUILT ENVIRONMENT:** Does the architecture, proximity, lighting, and use of space support culture change goals? Does the condition of the built environment send the mistaken message that desirable behavior is not important? Who will lead changes in built environment? What support will be needed to accomplish such changes?

- **COMMUNICATION AND INFORMATION:** How will people receive the information and updates needed to maintain desired behavior? Who will lead changes in communication strategies (e.g., newsletters, online forums, survey feedback, sharing of financial and customer satisfaction data)?

- **REWARDS AND RECOGNITION:** Are desired behaviors being rewarded and recognized by your group/organization? Are positive practices undermined through rewards for undesirable behavior?

- **RELATIONSHIPS:** Is there a connection between desired behaviors and finding friends and membership in work teams? How will the new desired behavior strengthen relationships?

- **LEARNING AND TRAINING:** Are people taught the skills they need to excel at practicing the desired behavior? Is training in undesired practices (such as taking safety shortcuts) being offered by mistake?

- **MODELING:** Are their suitable role models at all levels in the organization (i.e., across gender, age, ethnic groups, non-management, management)? How will we increase the visibility of people modeling desired behavior? Do leaders demonstrate positive practices in their own behavior? Are there people modeling undesirable behaviors? How can we reduce the visibility of negative role models?

- **PUSHBACK:** Is unhealthy behavior challenged? Does the culture pushback against desired behavior? How will we change confrontation and pushback (e.g., reprimands, demotions, pay cuts, firings) so it is better aligned with culture change goals?

- **ONBOARDING:** Does the group/organization have a reputation consistent with the culture change goal? Are people made aware that support for proactive mental health is a work benefit? Are new people made aware of all the programs and activities supporting the desired behavior? Are people assisted in their efforts to integrate desired behavior into their new roles and responsibilities?

- **TRADITIONS AND SYMBOLS:** Are there traditions and symbols associated with the desired behavior? Are there old traditions and symbols that might be adjusted so not to undermine the desired behavior? What new traditions and symbols could be established to support the culture change?

- **STORY AND NARRATIVE:** What stories are being told about the history and future of the organization or group? Who are the important characters? What lessons were learned about proactive mental health? Who were the heroes and villains? What does the outlook and future hold? How can these stories and narratives be modified to support the desired culture?

- **ROLES AND RESPONSIBILITIES:** What do managers do to address mental health concerns and to create proactive mental health cultures within their teams? What do employees do to support their mental health and the mental health of coworkers? What is the role of family and friends in supporting mental health? Are mental health counselors and human resources staff available to support mental health needs? What changes in roles and responsibilities will be needed to support the desired culture?

- **GOAL SETTING AND PLANNING:** What are the primary ways planning gets accomplished, and goals are set? In what ways, if at all, is employee mental health a part of the decision-making process? What could be done to include the proactive mental health goal in these considerations? What plans and benchmarks need to be established for progress at the individual, work team and organizational levels?

- **LAWS AND POLICIES:** What laws and policies have a bearing on the proactive mental health goal? Are there helpful policies and laws that need to become established?

All the touchpoints are already active in most settings. Your goal is to reduce or eliminate the influences that undermine the desired norm. Ideally, this is an alignment of existing influences rather than an entirely new manifestation of a touchpoint. So, for example, modifying existing training programs is better than creating an entirely new set of trainings. However, it may be useful to develop a new tradition in a setting that lacks traditions. The goal is to align sufficient influences and touchpoints to sustain the new norm. Changing just one touchpoint is unlikely to bring about sustained change because the influences of other touchpoints are likely to overwhelm the impact of that one touchpoint. The changes should be implemented in sufficient amount and at a pace that maintains momentum. While it is helpful to consider all the touchpoints, a tipping point can be achieved with as few as four changes to these powerful cultural influences.

Chapter 7

Provide Organizational Support for Purpose

"Efforts and courage are not enough without purpose and direction."

—John F. Kennedy

Purpose is a life-changing, life-sustaining building block of proactive mental health and organizational engagement. There are many ways to pursue a personal sense of purpose. Our personal purposes include such endeavors as artistic expression and connecting to social groups, work, religion, and family. There are also multiple ways organizations can support employees' sense of purpose.

What follows are 26 organizational strategies for supporting personal purpose. Each of the 26 strategies includes a list of design questions. The design questions can help you evaluate your current efforts and develop plans for using the strategy.

Likely, your group or organization is already engaged in some of these strategies. Celebrate these strengths. As you read the descriptions of each strategy, identify approaches that will amplify your current efforts. Your goal is to increase the quantity and quality of support for purpose. This could be accomplished by improving upon strategies already in place. You are also likely to see new strategies would complement your group. These additions could be organized into lists of short-term and long-term goals for supporting purpose.

1. Provide Regular Feedback

Feedback is more than a way to remedy mistakes: feedback also acknowledges effort. Such recognition is an important source of purpose. There are few things more demoralizing and confusing than working without feedback. Most feedback should answer the question: How am I doing? Here are a few tips for effective feedback. To the extent possible, feedback should:

- Be primarily positive. Recognize work that is done well. Our strengths help us move forward.

- Be given at frequent intervals. Don't wait until your criticism is no longer about recent behavior.

- Be specific about the behavior, using recent examples.

- Allow for two-way communication. Use face-to-face communication when possible.

- Be offered in a private setting, to guard against embarrassment.

- Connect guidance with the broader purposes of the group or organization.

Design Questions: Regular Feedback

- Do we offer people adequate training in how to give and receive constructive feedback?

- Are we collecting the right information needed to provide feedback?

- Do we share information people need to set personal and team goals?

- Do we give feedback at sufficient intervals to keep people abreast of their performance?

- Do we give feedback in a format that allows for two-way communication?

- Do people view feedback favorably and as a constructive part of achieving the group's—or organization's—purpose?

2. Create a System for Peers to Honor One Another's Efforts

Acknowledgement by peers is an important source of purpose. When peers take notice of each other, there is a special sense of accomplishment that can only come from receiving acknowledgement from others who have taken on similar roles, tasks, and responsibilities. The bonds and friendship between peers also add weight and meaning to the acknowledgement.

Design Questions: Honoring Peers' Efforts

- Do we have a system for peers to recognize each other's efforts? For example, you could offer a recognition system that is triggered when co-workers report someone has done exceptional work.

- Are people sharing positive feedback with each other?

- Is peer recognition normal in our organization?

3. Involve People in Decisions Affecting Them

People should have as much discretion as possible in how they work or contribute. When people have an active role in planning their efforts, they are more receptive to those efforts—they own them. Such involvement enhances the sense of personal accomplishment and purpose. Empowerment takes the form of knowledge, collaboration, and permission. People must understand the factors influencing their efforts. They should be given the wherewithal to work to the best of their abilities. This includes permission to enlist the support of others.

Design Questions: Involving People in Decisions

- Do people have all the information that pertains to their efforts?

- Do they get to ask questions and dig deep into details?

- Do we encourage people to work together to improve their efforts?

- Do we give people permission to do their jobs in ways they think will produce the best results?

- Are people regularly asked to provide input before goals and plans are set?

- Is it clear whether people are being asked for their input or being given a full choice in how or if change occurs?

- Do we try to limit or avoid decisions that go against the preferences of those most affected?

4. Set Challenging Goals for Individuals, Groups, and the Organization

Meeting challenges directly fuels purpose and builds resilience. Organizations without short-term and long-term goals can feel adrift with no reminder or barometer toward purpose with smaller milestones. Goals (individual, group and organizational) should focus, energize, and engage people. Goals are more meaningful when challenges are clear and buy-in exists from those supporting the goals.

Design Questions: Setting Goals

- Have there been sufficient opportunities to set goals and identify steps toward their achievement?

- Have we provided guidance for setting goals that are a stretch, yet are within the capacity of the group?

- Is there a solid mix of individual and group goals?

- Have we identified clear benchmarks to signal we are making progress?

- Does the plan make sense to those responsible for carrying it out?

- Do people recognize how and when progress will be measured?

- Do people have the freedom and authority they need to accomplish goals?

- Are priorities clear?

5. Follow Through on Current Goals before Taking on New Ones

A sense of accomplishment is more likely when well-developed plans are carried to fruition. Sticking to a plan reduces confusion and engenders teamwork. Ideally, new goals and strategies are tackled only after completing or retiring current ones. At a minimum, a revised plan should reflect consideration for prior plans and goals.

Design Questions: Follow Through on Current Goals Before Taking on New Ones

- Have we reviewed old plans and goals to tie up loose ends, celebrate accomplishments and include lessons learned in any new plan?

- Have we given people an opportunity to provide input about new ideas and goals?

- Have we given adequate thought to next steps and the resources required to achieve them?

- Is there a feedback loop that will show follow-through and results?

6. Help People See the Fruit of Their Efforts

Many products and services are made in stages. People involved in the initial or later stages may not observe the complete process or end product. Find ways to help people bear witness to the fruits of their labor and the benefits and joy being delivered. This connection to end use will increase the sense of purpose in the work done at each stage.

Design Questions: Help People See the Fruit of Their Efforts

- How can we encourage all those involved in the creation of a product or service to experience it for themselves?

- How can people receive end-user feedback or actually meet the end users so they can see and hear about the benefits derived from the products or services?

7. Build Legacies

Leaving a legacy is the crown jewel of purpose, most noticeable when employees near retirement or move onto a different assignment. People coming to the end of their responsibilities may feel they are just waiting for their time to pass. They may be physically present, but psychologically checked out.

The goal of creating a legacy can add purpose throughout employees' engagement. They can recognize how their efforts contribute over time to a positive story of organizational growth and success.

Design Questions: Build Legacies

- Do people feel they are part of an important ongoing story? Are they familiar with the history and hoped-for future of this group or organizational story?

- Do veteran employees know their skills and experiences are valued? Do they have an opportunity to pass these along to newer employees through programs such as mentoring or on-the-job training?

- Do we ask employees approaching transitions, including retirement, to help guide the future direction and assist with the transition?

8. Limit Interruptions

Maybe you've heard the lament, "If they'd just let me do my job!" Team meetings and measurement have their place, but in almost all cases, such disruptions should be kept to a minimum. Management oversight and input can be helpful, but it needs to be unobtrusive. Some tasks require undivided attention over a sustained period. Schedules should reflect this need for focus. Establish boundaries that give people the physical and mental space to do their best work.

Design Questions: Limit Interruptions

- Do we give people the time and space they need to work in an uninterrupted fashion?

- Do we support effective workflow by limiting meetings, offline organizational functions, and other activities?

9. Support Professional Development

Acquiring knowledge and skills is a far-reaching source of purpose both at work and outside of work. Every job and task can be done to a high standard. This is as true for CEOs as it is for hourly employees, for full-time and contract and gig workers—and across all categories of employees.

Periodic training, continuing education, certifications, and introducing state-of-the-art work tools help refresh the work experience and fosters professional pride. Empowering people to innovate and determine the best way to achieve tasks also support professionalism. Career ladders, mentoring programs and graduated pay scales play a role. Memberships in professional organizations and unions can also nurture a professional identity. Regular customer feedback also helps maintain professional standards.

Design Questions: Professional Development

- Do we encourage learning?
- Do people receive the training needed to strengthen their skills, and the most up-to-date information related to their work?
- Are there career paths and other ways to honor new abilities and professional growth?
- Are tools and equipment up-to-date and well-maintained?
- Do we support people being a part of organizations associated with their work?

10. Support Reflection and Centering

Stress and time pressures from overload and clutter can distract from and obscure purpose. Decluttering, efficient scheduling and setting limits are all important for focus. They help people become centered and stay centered.

Voluntary timeouts (taking a few deep breaths, getting up from your workstation, or whatever calms your nerves) help us find the space we need to reflect and tune into what is important. When we feel harried, on the other hand, it's difficult to benefit from otherwise pleasant activities. Regular exercise and mindfulness practices help us quiet and refresh our minds. Regularly scheduled days off, vacations, and sabbaticals also make it more likely that we can re-center and focus when working.

Design Questions: Reflection and Centering

- Do we encourage people to set reasonable limits on their commitments?

- Do we limit clutter, noise, and chaos so people can better tune into their purposeful activities?

- Do we provide the time and place for people to clear their minds or center themselves through activities such as meditation, prayer and exercise?

- Do we provide counseling and other support services for those seeking assistance with managing stress, addressing feelings of being overwhelmed, or getting sufficient rest?

- Do we offer vacations and/or sabbaticals that allow for renewal and to refocus?

11. Help Make Sense of Disruptive or Unexpected Events

Sometimes people are confronted by events so unfamiliar or unexpected that disorientation and anxiety may occur. Such disruptions can result from international, national, or local events, and may be relatively large (such as war, acts of terror, or natural disaster) or small (such as the introduction of new work methods). Leaders must be ready to interpret events, as well as call upon outside experts to help calm the waters. After disruptions, it is important to focus on the best ways forward, reestablish confidence, and regroup around shared purpose and goals, both personal and organizational.

Design Questions: Making Sense of Disruptive or Unexpected Events

- Do people have the support they need to get through crises that challenge their personal purpose or shared purposes?

- Do people have access to support groups, employee assistance services or counselors?

- Do people have opportunities to meet to share, discuss, and move toward making sense of catastrophic events or other disruptions? For instance, are there memorial gatherings or ways the community can pull together to grieve what has been lost and assess best steps toward healing and recovery?

- Do people have ways to help each other during disruptions or after tragedies?

- When tragedy or disruptions occur, is there full disclosure of what happened and the implications?

- Have we taken steps to prevent additional occurrences of such events?

- After tragedies or dramatic changes, do we help people see the path forward and reestablish hope for the future?

12. Engage Neglected or Forgotten Stakeholders

Most groups and organizations serve a variety of stakeholders. For example, the stakeholders of a typical business include current employees, past employees, employees' dependents (particularly in the case of benefits), shareholders/owners, managers, suppliers, customers, and the surrounding neighborhoods, towns, and state.

These stakeholders should be involved in key decisions, particularly if those decisions will have a direct impact on them. Keeping communication lines open and taking various constituencies into consideration builds mutual trust and a connection to the organization's future; that connection can be important to stakeholders' sense of meaning and purpose. This is particularly apparent when the identity of a community is connected to an organization. Such was the case when Ben & Jerry's was a Vermont-based company. Vermonters felt a special connection with Ben & Jerry that was at least partially lost when the company was purchased by Unilever, a multinational corporation.

Design Questions: Engaging Stakeholders

- Who are all the stakeholders and how do we connect to them?

- Do we honor the connection we have with all our stakeholders?

- When making important decisions, have we taken into consideration all the stakeholders' needs?

13. Write or Update the Mission and Vision Statements

Agreeing on shared purposes and taking stands together can be important sources of purpose. When they are properly reinforced and celebrated, shared purposes can be valuable reference points for effective decision-making. Adding statements of purpose, such as a mission statement, vision statement, credo, principles, or core values, may help refine the organization's overarching purpose and engage people in supporting it. Such statements address foundation questions, such as:

- Why are we here?

- What most defines and distinguishes our products and services?

- How do we intend to treat our customers, each other, and society?

- What will the future hold for our organization? To what extent can we shape that future? What are the major variables?

- Whom do we serve as primary and other stakeholders?

- What, in other words, makes us special?

When creating such statements of common purpose, keep in mind these are living agreements serving as a mirror in which all members of your organization can see themselves. Credible and useful statements are based on clarity, sincerity, conviction, and brevity.

Design Questions: Write or Update the Mission and Vision Statements

- Can people see their own personal values reflected in the stated values, purposes and intentions of the group or organization?

- Are these documents sufficiently clear, inspirational, and actionable (i.e., people can see how they apply to key decisions)?

- Do we update the core documents at regular intervals, and are people sufficiently involved in the process?

14. Offer a Compelling Story

Some groups and organizations are fortunate to have been part of a compelling or inspirational story. For example, M.D. Anderson and Memorial Sloan-Kettering have worked for decades to find cures for cancer. Many people have dedicated their lives to these efforts; in so doing, they have served an important purpose and become part of history. Groups and organizations of all kinds can support purpose by retelling a compelling story about what they've achieved and how people have contributed to it.

Design Questions: Offer a Compelling Story

- Have our products or services fulfilled a valued need? Providing an excellent product or service can be an important purpose. You can tell a story about developing and delivering important products or services.

- Have we achieved outstanding results? Going above and beyond is story with added purpose.

- Have we innovated? Being a part of the story about innovation in your field can add purpose.

- Have we done something altruistic? The story of helping others, of making their lives better, adds purpose.

- Have we overcome a setback or challenge? The story of coming together to meet challenges is an important source of purpose.

- Have we sufficiently shared how particularly visionary or creative people contributed to our success?

- Have we found ways to extend our story into the future? Explaining how your organization is continuing to build upon its story keeps purposes fresh and relevant.

- Have we provided a steady source of well-paying jobs and benefits? Helping people provide for their loved ones and enjoy economic security are important purposes.

15. Connect to Future Generations

Family connections are an important source of purpose in many people's lives. People also find meaning in supporting future generations. Some organizations find ways to celebrate families young and old. This can be as simple as including family members in holiday events and retreats. Other organizations build a special bond with families by employing multiple family members. Another strategy is to find charitable causes that benefit future generations. Groups and organizations sometimes support schools with scholarships, internships, and information about how to pursue careers.

Design Questions: Connect to Future Generations

- Have we invited family members or young people in general to join our group or organization?
- Do we have a formal or informal mentoring program for bringing younger generations into the group or organization?
- Have we found a way to support young people?

16. Support Nature and Sustainability

Protecting the environment is a purpose. Organizations and groups can find ways to reduce their negative environmental impact. Many people find purpose in joining with others to advocate for and participate in environmental stewardship and restoration. Time spent outdoors in natural settings reestablishes a psychological connection to living things. Time in nature can be uplifting and meaningful. The design of our living spaces at home, in workplaces and in the community can enhance connections with nature. Access to sunlight, fresh air, plants, and animals are links to nature. Organizations can help these connections be part of the daily routine by supporting work breaks, alternate modes of transportation and recreational activities to bring people into closer contact with nature.

Design Questions: Support Nature and Sustainability

- Are we minimizing our negative impact on the natural environment?

- Do we do enough to live and work in ways that support the environment?

- Have we designed our spaces and allotted sufficient time to help people maintain a connection with nature?

17. Champion a Cause or Take a Principled Stand

Sometimes organizations and groups adopt a special cause. Such support for a cause can add purpose. Examples include raising funds for worthy causes and working in other ways to combat diseases, reduce homelessness and/or hunger, improve high school graduation rates, etc.

Sometimes groups and organizations do things seemingly at odds with financial or other interests in efforts to promote the greater good (an example would be the dental associations support for fluoridated drinking water). Taking a principled stand can generate a sense of purpose.

Design Questions: Champion a Cause or Take a Stand

- Are there times when the organization or group does some things on principle because it is the right thing to do, even when it might undercut other goals? Have we explained and acknowledged these principled stands?

- Do we support causes or charities? Have people been involved in selecting these causes or charities? Are people able to contribute to these efforts?

- Do we encourage people to take principled stands and support causes they find worthwhile?

- Are people aware of the causes their peers support?

18. Support Wellness

Caring for the health and wellbeing of people can be an important purpose. Wellness is often expressed as overall physical, emotional, social, and economic wellbeing. Many groups and organizations support healthy lifestyle practices.

Wellness initiatives encourage expanded awareness, skill development, peer support, supportive physical environments, and reduced barriers to positive practices. Some groups and organizations work to create wellness cultures that align priorities, norms, peer support, policies, and social climates to support wellness.

Through wellness initiatives, groups and organizations show they care for their own people and others. In addition to supporting the purpose of taking care of oneself, wellness initiatives also offer ways for people to help others. Altruism is another source of purpose. Wellness encourages and facilitates mental focus, stamina, and a positive outlook. In addition, the challenge of being at one's best is a compelling purpose.

Design Questions: Support Wellness

- Does our group or organization show it really cares about peoples' wellbeing?

- Do we fully inform people about how wellness can improve health, wellbeing, and personal performance?

- Do we foster peer support for wellness by, for example, offering team activities and buddy systems? Do these peer support efforts include co-workers, friends, housemates, and family?

- Do executives, managers, and wellness champions support wellness by being role models, aligning policies with wellness, reducing resource barriers to pursuing wellness, and celebrating peoples' efforts?

19. Encourage Mutual Interest Groups

Professional associations, clubs, teams, and unions are important sources of purpose. They can add to camaraderie and a sense of pride. Such mutually beneficial associations strengthen job stability, intragroup integrity and trust. The activities of such associations strengthen friendships and opportunities for family connections and enable people to share interests outside of work. Many are highly participatory and volunteer led; service to these groups can be yet another source of purpose.

Design Questions: Encourage Mutual Interest Groups

- Have we assisted in the formation and support of associations, clubs, teams, and unions?

- Do these interest groups provide opportunities for members to volunteer and lead?

- Do they encourage people to know one another better and share more about their lives outside of work?

- Do they enhance pride and respect by members for each other and their roles within the group or organization?

20. Encourage Creative Expression

Creative expression is another potential source of meaning. In the case of actors, writers and visual artists, such creativity is fundamental to peoples' roles. However, including a creative aspect in any role is possible. A parent, for example, could make parenting highly creative by developing unusual or elaborate family traditions. Employees could invent fun names for new products that delight customers.

Design Questions: Encourage Creative Expression

- Do we encourage people to express their creative sides?

- Are people able to share their creative works and/ or to experience the arts?

- Do we support people in developing creative interests outside of responsibilities associated with our group or organization?

21. Develop Win-Win Solutions

Groups and organizations can take steps for enabling people to find common ground, resolving unwarranted tradeoffs, and advancing win-win thinking. In many settings, two roles or groups are mistakenly seen as being natural enemies. Examples include teachers and administrators in schools, doctors and nurses in medical settings, and managers and workers in organizations. Such animosities, not surprisingly, detract from the mission by sowing confusion, undermining enthusiasm, reducing cooperation, and distracting all parties. A similar challenge is evident when different philosophical positions or simple priorities separate factions in fruitless ideological struggles. A medical example: should we emphasize treating the sick, preventing illness, or promoting wellness? All three are mutually beneficial. Progress in one area increases the likelihood of positive outcomes in the other two areas.

Design Questions: Develop Win-Win Solutions

- Have we identified unproductive, competing disputes or ideas that exist between groups?

- Have stakeholders had an opportunity to suggest "win-win" approaches to better align competing constituencies?

- Have we developed win-win alternatives showing how success in one area can enhance prospects for the other? At minimum, have we explored and challenged the perceived tradeoffs between positive outcomes?

22. Maintain Economic Transparency

Open disclosure about the big financial picture empowers employees. When appreciated as necessary, employees will support corrective actions. Sometimes they will do much more, such as come up with valuable business strategies. Employees are usually willing to pitch in, give back and do what it takes to save the organization if they feel consulted and otherwise treated well. Being a part of guiding an organization through hard times is a great source of purpose.

Some organizations improve their financial picture but remain in an economic crisis mode. This necessitates only low-cost or no-cost ideas. Many purposes require new funds or at least a substantial initial investment. Let people know when conditions have improved, and optional investments are once again prudent.

Design Questions: Maintain Economic Transparency

- Do we, or will we, remain true to purposes, in good times and bad, during the calm and the storms of changing conditions and circumstances over time?

- Does the group or organization entrust its people with a full and accurate understanding of its current financial health and future prospects?

- During times of financial troubles, do we enlist people in developing and carrying out strategies for addressing the economic picture? When (and if) the going gets tough, will we get going?

- Do we share openly about improving financial conditions, how we will redress cutbacks, and how we will handle new opportunities to invest? Will we celebrate such improvement, including recognition for the sacrifices made to address the financial challenges?

23. Provide Adequate Compensation

Almost all workers view pay as important to their purpose. Salary and benefits reflect an ongoing effort to meet financial obligations and to fund future independence, pleasures, and generosity. Compensation enables employees to support their families, pursue creative interests, and contribute to the community. Suitable compensation underwrites being part of the larger economic system.

Adequate compensation enables employees and their families to thrive. Too little pay, and they may have to seek additional work. Added work often interferes with desired purposeful activities, among them family time. Financial worries distract from purpose.

Adequate compensation and benefits also provide a financial buffer that enables psychological security, protects against the calamities, unforeseen illnesses, and setbacks we all face. Adequate compensation enables people to meet the predictable demands of insurance, vacations, a child's education, etc. Benefits such as paid family leave, sick days, health insurance and retirement plans support our capacity to manage and plan ahead.

Employees find it much easier to focus on meaningful

work when wolves in the form of financial woes and demands are not growling at the door.

Design Questions: Provide Adequate Compensation

- Is base compensation adequate for living a good life free of worries about basic needs?

- Does compensation provide insurance or a safety net for unanticipated expenses?

- Do people have the discretionary income needed to pursue hobbies, altruistic pursuits, and other interests?

24. Recognize Non-Financial Compensation

Appreciation of the intangible benefits of work is a source of purpose. Similarly, purpose declines when non-monetary benefits are underappreciated. Work should be seen as delivering more than a paycheck. Opportunities to form and maintain friendships are benefits of work, as are chances for expressing creativity and helping others. Attention should be given to the full value of intangible benefits.

Design Questions: Non-Financial Compensation

- Do we give enough attention to all the benefits of work, beyond pay?

- Do we give enough consideration to non-monetary benefits when we set policies and procedures?

25. Tailor Benefits to Individual Purpose

Each of us is attracted to a different set of purposes, and purposes change over the course of our lives. Benefits and responsibilities should reflect the dynamic nature of purpose. For example, a new parent will need more job flexibility to accommodate the needs of an infant. Flexible benefits can also support varied interests such as music, athletics, and continuing education.

Design Questions: Tailor Benefits to Individual Purpose

- Does the structure of work rules and benefits accommodate varied purposes?
- Do we build policies to accommodate different purposes for all ages in our population, as well as other groupings?

26. Promote Work-Life Balance

There are times when a commitment to excellence and customer needs demands an intense focus and lots of extra effort. These busy times can be a rich source of purpose. However, it is important to limit such times. Giving up work-life balance should not become the new normal. Predictable work hours and reasonable workloads enable people to pursue purposes outside of work, such as connecting with family and friends.

Design Questions: Work-Life Balance

- Have we made it clear that intense work schedules are temporary? After a time when more work intensity is required, do we encourage people to rebalance and reestablish sustainable workflows?

- Have we put systems in place to increase the likelihood people will have predictable work hours that preserve time to engage in interests outside of work?

- Are workloads and responsibilities at reasonable levels allowing people to not feel pressured to compromise important responsibilities they have outside of work?

- Do we encourage work breaks and vacations so people can recharge and reconnect to all their interests, work-related and otherwise?

Finding the Right Mix of Purpose Strategies

Don't be overwhelmed by the 26 strategies identified. Remember, this is not a to-do list. Instead, examine each strategy as an opportunity. Take your time; the power of each strategy requires care and attention. Add one or two to the mix. Determine which takes root. Don't consider adopting them all at once.

Your choice of strategies should be based on numerous factors, including their cost and complexity. Some strategies such as updating the mission statement or calling more attention to non-financial rewards are relatively low cost. Other strategies such as providing adequate compensation require a substantial financial commitment. However, fair compensation may be a prerequisite to gaining traction with other important purpose strategies.

These purpose strategies can also strengthen the social climate (see Chapter 5). The sense of community, shared vision, and positive outlook greatly enhances the capacity to achieve individual and collective sense of purpose. Revisit the strategies list in this chapter to see how the strategies could be used to lessen social discord and bring people closer together.

Chapter 8

Make Proactive Mental Health Transformational

"For every complex problem there is an answer that is clear, simple, and wrong."

—H. L. MENCKEN

WE FLOURISH CHAPTERS 3, 4 and 5 examine the six culture building blocks. The complexity of culture makes it highly resistant to change. Changing culture can be like punching into a soft pillow. If you don't make sufficient change to the six culture building blocks, your efforts will be only temporary rather than transformative. Many leaders under-estimate the power of culture in undermining their favorite ideas. For example, they might falsely believe providing information about mental health is sufficient to bring about proactive mental health practices. "If only that were true, many more Americans would be at their desired weight. We would all naturally be basking in happy and healthy lives without the need for support.

Systematic Culture Change

The complexity of culture requires a step-by-step and ongoing approach to change. Such an approach offers a roadmap for involving people in co-creating the new culture and provides a system of continuous improvement. In adopting a step-by-step approach, culture change can be broken down into manageable tasks.

In Chapter 3, I explained the word "culture" originated from the farming concept of cultivation. The goal is to create a social environment (fertile ground) that will make it easy to adopt proactive mental health attitudes and behavior (healthy products). The cycle of preparing the soil, planting the seed, nurturing the growing crop, and harvesting is also analogous to successful culture change. In the vein of being a skilled farmer, your job is to make the conditions right for nurturing proactive mental health. Your team's success largely depends on your ability to adjust your culture-building efforts, so they match the conditions under which you operate. The culture-change process involves four seasons.

Four Seasons of Systematic Culture Change

Season	Culture Change Goal
Winter (plan)	**Analyze the current culture:** Set culture-change goals and develop leadership support.
Spring (plant)	**Introduce goals and get buy-in:** Explain what was learned in your analysis and ask your team to pitch in.
Summer (cultivate)	**Align touchpoints:** Address day-to-day cultural influences such as modeling, training, workplace policies, communications, and traditions to support the desired culture.
Fall (harvest)	**Track and celebrate success:** Assess progress, improve upon strategies, and celebrate achievements. Then begin to develop the next goals for a new cycle of change.

The Culture-Change Process

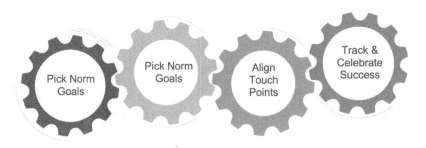

The culture-change process involves four phases. Phase I consists of developing an understanding of the current culture, setting goals, and developing leadership commitment. In Phase II, the vision for the new culture can be planted among the members of the culture. In Phase III, programs, policies, and procedures are aligned so that the new culture can take root. In Phase IV, change is assessed, progress is celebrated, and new goals are developed. This virtuous cycle of culture change builds a proactive mental health culture.

This is a continuous process. The proactive mental health needs of your organization will always change. Make the culture change process an annual tradition embedded in long-term plans and watch your organization's commitment to proactive team mental health flourish. Develop the capacity to set new culture goals and systematically bring about needed change.

Phase I
Preparation: Analysis, Objective Setting, and Leadership Development

The first phase of project development establishes a clear picture of the current situation, sets specific and measurable objectives, and commits leaders to a vision for change. These activities serve to tailor the change process to the problem and setting. Phase I activities provide the groundwork for the broad-scale introduction and integration of the change process. The analysis covers three broad categories of information: performance, programmatic, and cultural.

Performance Analysis

Performance data encompass bottom-line financial and behavioral measures. Sometimes this information is readily available, but often, additional measures must be developed. For example, a project designed to create new norms for physical activity should base its goals on what the science asserts about the level and types of activities that produce health benefits. Some measure of activity would need to be introduced to track progress.

Performance Analysis: Strategic Design Questions

- How will behavior be measured?
- What are the human and economic costs of current behavior?
- What new behaviors are likely to produce the largest human benefit and economic returns?
- How will the economic and human impact be measured?
- What is the current success rate in achieving desired behavior? For example, in the case of a goal for physical activity, what is the long-term success rate for achieving active lifestyles?

Programmatic Analysis

Every setting and group handles change differently. Some groups need change to occur at a rapid pace, while others call for a more gradual approach. In some settings, those in power need to lead the change process, while in other settings, change only works when those at the bottom of the power hierarchy demand change. Programmatic analysis examines how change efforts should be organized to maximize the likelihood of success.

Programmatic Analysis: Strategic Design Questions

- Who is already engaged in achieving the current goal? In the case of culture change goal for physical activity, who attempted to become more physically active in the past year?

- How will the past influence the change process?

- Who will need to be involved in the change process?

- Who should play a leadership role in steering the change process?

- What should the structure, composition, and purposes of committees and/or task forces be?

- What is the best strategy for introducing the change process?

- What is the best timeline for project development?

Cultural Analysis

Both qualitative and quantitative cultural measures help guide the change effort. A questionnaire can ask members of the group or organization for their perceptions of cultural support. Such a quantitative measure can ask participants to rate their level of agreement that a given cultural influence is present. People can be asked about their level of agreement that a norm has been established. Examples of culture surveys are provided chapters four, six and seven.

Interviews, observation and focus groups are qualitative cultural measures. Individual and group interviews can gather input on the best approach to addressing cultural support for a desired norm. For example, if the culture goal is regular physical activity, people can suggest the best approach to rewarding physical activity. Participants can also offer insight into past efforts to address the desired behavior.

Cultural Analysis: Strategic Design Questions

- What will be done to make the culture change goals among the top priorities within the culture?

- What are the current norms? What are the key norm goals?

- How do cultural touchpoints influence behavior? How will cultural touchpoints be aligned with culture change goals?

- What are the current sources, levels, and quality of peer support? How might peer support play a constructive role in supporting change efforts?

- How strong is the current sense of community, shared vision, and positive outlook? How will the initiative foster a good social climate?

Leadership Commitment

Obtaining leadership commitment is useful throughout the culture change process. Ideally, the leader will show this commitment through being a role model and by disclosing personal proactive mental health goals. Leaders can also commit organizational resources to the initiative. Ideally, leaders would express their enthusiasm when employees are introduced to culture change effort (see Phase II).

Leadership Commitment: Strategic Design Questions

- How should leaders call attention to the economic and human costs of the current culture?

- How should leaders state the intended benefits of the culture change effort?

- What is the best strategy for reviewing past failed approaches to change? How will leaders recognize the role of culture in those failed efforts?

- How will leaders get an opportunity to experience the desired culture? Will this happen at a retreat or through field visits to other cultures?

- How will leaders commit to a specific timeline and cost structure for project development?

- How will leaders help identify benchmarks of success?

- What is the best way to teach leaders skills and concepts that will make them useful in the culture change process? (For example, they could learn how to share the project vision, serve as role models, align policies, and celebrate progress.)

- How will leaders link their personal values and vision to the project?

Phase II
Involvement: Systems Introduction

The second phase introduces members of the culture to the project vision and invites participation in the change process.

Although printed materials and visual media can be useful in getting the word out, the best Phase II efforts usually include an experiential, dynamic workshop. The workshop provides a forum for relating project goals to personal values and experiences. Most workshops are designed so participants can visualize and experience the desired culture. The workshops often have a three-part agenda: understanding, identifying, and changing. Discussions of these subjects follow.

Understanding

Members of the culture should become familiar with the key lessons of Phase I. Such lessons often include the current human and economic costs of the existing culture. These costs are presented in terms of their impact on individuals as well as their impact on the organization, community, and society.

It is also useful to review the history of past change

attempts that failed. What were their strengths, and why did they fall short? Perhaps these attempts failed because they focused on a single factor (e.g., laws in the alcohol prohibition movement), or because they did not adequately involve people (e.g., a memo from management), or because they were unsystematic (e.g., they relied on a campaign or on a single seminar experience).

Participants would also benefit from an understanding of the power of culture, sometimes addressed by discussing the impact of cultural norms. Most norms go unexamined. As a result, it is eye-opening to see how our own behavior is influenced by norms. This understanding is useful in reducing the likelihood of placing the blame on individuals. The discussion can also be instrumental in helping people realize they will need to work together for meaningful, lasting results.

Finally, developing an understanding of the follow-up available to support the new norms will be beneficial. The cultural analysis revealed ways to better align cultural touchpoints (see Chapter 7). Workshop participants will learn how key touchpoints will be aligned with the proactive mental health culture goals.

Understanding: Strategic Design Questions

- How will the economic and human costs of the current culture be explained? What will be said about the impact of the culture on the individual? What will be said about the impact on the group, organization, or society?

- How will past change attempts be explained? What lessons about culture change can be integrated into this explanation?

- What is the best mechanism to teach about the power of culture to influence behavior? Can the discussion of culture be summarized in such a way that people will understand the futility of negative blame-placing and realize the importance of joining together in finding a lasting solution?

- What was learned from the analysis of cultural influences? What key influences will be aligned first and why?

Identifying

Leaders share their vision for program outcomes. They also thank workshop attendees for their participation. An assessment useful for setting personal and team goals is provided. Individual and team goals are established.

Identifying: Strategic Design Questions

- How will participants assess their own behavior?

- How will individual goals be set?

- How will individuals track their progress?

- How will teams establish shared behavioral goals?

- How will teams be given feedback on their progress?

Changing

Individuals and teams should be given opportunities to develop change plans. To facilitate this planning process, participants are made aware of what is being done to bring about sustained change. Frequently, this information is presented in a menu of follow-up activities. New ideas are also generated.

Changing: Strategic Design Questions

- What format will individual action plans take? Will specific action steps be recommended?

- What format will group action plans take? Will specific action steps be recommended?

- How will people be informed about the availability of programs and materials supporting their goals?

- Will people be invited to participate in committees and task forces? If so, how will this be handled?

- How will new ideas and suggested changes in current plans be shared? How will this information be integrated into the change process?

Phase III
Systems Integration

To assure success, change must take place on multiple levels. Phase III Focuses on individual efforts, peer support, organizational support, and leadership development.

Individual-Level Integration

Self-help change initiatives play an integral role in culture-change projects. Self-help activities include individual therapy and coaching, attending seminars, watching videos, reading books and pamphlets, and more recently, using computer applications. For example, such activities can help people develop psychological and social skills needed to work with others. Increased awareness about personal strengths and styles can foster individual initiative and creativity.

The most effective self-help programs engage people in developing their own individual initiative while also finding or building supportive environments. Self-help materials and programs must reinforce the symbiotic relationship between personal and cultural change. For example, a self-help program could suggest that participants assess those aspects of their cultural environments standing in the way of their personal success.

Individual Level Integration: Strategic Design Questions

- What format(s) should self-help material and support take (e.g., counseling, videos, pamphlets, newsletter, apps, etc.)?

- How will those involved in self-help activities be given opportunities to share their experiences?

- How will self-help programs include a role for cultural support?

Peer-Level Integration

People often think of peer support in terms of special cause-centered groups such as Alcoholics Anonymous and Weight Watchers. Support group members share their common experiences with a given problem behavior or experience. Such groups play important roles in supporting individuals through difficult personal changes. Groups make it possible to share and exchange solutions and/or ways to get through, endure, and triumph.

Peer-level integration efforts also address the needs of ongoing, naturally occurring social networks such as work teams, families, and friends. Unlike support groups, which tend to be time limited, natural social networks continue to provide support for years and sometimes for a lifetime.

Peer integration efforts are designed to increase the quantity and improve the quality of support. For example, family, friends, and coworkers can learn skills for being effective role models, working through relapse or celebrating success (see Chapter 4 for a discussion of peer support skills).

Peer-Level Integration: Strategic Design Questions

- What support groups, if any, should be organized? How long and how often will they meet?

- How will friends be involved in the change process? What training might friends receive?

- How will family members or housemates be involved in the change process? What training might these people receive?

- How will co-workers support each other? What training in peer support will coworkers need?

Organization-Level Integration

The focus of organization-level integration is the alignment of cultural touchpoints (also known as formal and informal policies and procedures). The alignment of cultural touchpoints is discussed in Chapter 6. The goal is to align enough of the 14 touchpoints to sustain the new culture. The changes should be implemented in sufficient amount and at a pace that maintains momentum. While it is helpful to consider all the touchpoints, a tipping point can be achieved with as few as four changes to these powerful cultural influences.

Typically, these efforts are carried out by a task force and through leadership mandate. In larger organizations, aligning cultural touchpoints tends to be the responsibility of the human resources department in conjunction with middle management.

Organizational-Level Integration: Strategic Design Questions

- Have informal influences (i.e., not written into policies and programs) been sufficiently addressed?

- Have the people with the knowledge and power to make these changes been sufficiently involved in making these changes?

- Have we addressed existing programs and policies to avoid creating an entire new layer or list of programs and policies on top of the old ones?

- Have we aligned enough touchpoints to bring about sustained change?

Leadership-Level Integration

Leaders play important roles in consistently articulating a vision of success. Leaders are also instrumental in inspiring commitment, recognizing contributions, designating needed resources, and ensuring plans are followed through to completion.

Many organizations establish committees, task forces and champion groups to lead the change process. Most culture change programs train these leaders and help to develop new leadership roles.

Leadership-Level Integration: Strategic Design Questions

- How will formal leadership at all levels (i.e., executives, managers, and supervisors) be involved in supporting the culture change effort?

- What skills will leaders need to successfully model their commitment to desired change?

- What new leadership roles might be necessary to bring about desired change? How will these new leaders be trained?

- How will leaders foster a climate that supports change?

Phase IV
Sustainability: Ongoing Evaluation, Renewal and Extension

During the fourth phase of project development performance, programmatic and cultural measures are repeated for evaluation purposes. Successes are celebrated. A determination is made as to what additional changes are needed to solidify the change. A plan for ongoing evaluation is devised. Lessons learned are incorporated for addressing future proactive mental health goals.

Phase IV efforts must provide sufficient opportunity to celebrate accomplishments. Avoid the tendency of many cultures to focus on what has not been achieved, thus discounting successes. Instead, celebration efforts can combine internal recognition with external public acclaim. Frequently, Phase IV activities include the publication of project findings.

Project extension plays an important role in culture change. It may be possible, for example, to assist other organizations or teams to take on similar proactive mental health goals. Perhaps most importantly, such extensions efforts help establish support in the broader culture. Change in the broader culture makes it easier to maintain local progress, and assisting others generates new ideas for the home front.

Evaluation, Renewal and Extension: Strategic Design Questions

- What performance, programmatic and cultural goals were achieved?

- What new goals, if any, should be set?

- How will accomplishments be celebrated?

- What steps need to be taken to maintain and deepen cultural change?

- How can lessons from this experience be shared with other groups, organizations, or communities?

- How can lessons from this experience be applied to other cultural problems?

Futureproofing for Proactive Mental Health

The four phases are likely to achieve important proactive mental health results. Using such as systematic approach also builds your team's capacity to achieve future proactive mental health goals. Also highly likely, your team will need to address evolving, and perhaps unforeseen, working conditions. The best culture this year is unlikely to meet your team's needs next year. For example, the safe behaviors primary in the early days of the COVID-19 pandemic evolved as vaccines and treatments became available. The disorientation and alienation that some stay-at-home workers experienced was likely to dissipate as new cultural expectations for such blended employment emerged. In general, the stressors currently existing with a tight labor force are unlikely to always dominate working conditions and business decisions. Although adopting a systematic approach takes considerable energy and focus, the system will build capacity to achieve future change goals.

The Future of Proactive Mental Health

On this day, it wouldn't be farfetched to imagine a dystopian future. It's a bit depressing.

- The climate is steadily warming. Wildfires, droughts, and floods are dislocating entire populations. Animals are going extinct at an alarming rate.

- A war is raging in Ukraine. Putin's army is carpet bombing entire cities. No one knows how to stop a mad man with nuclear bombs.

- It does not feel safe to go out. Few people are wearing masks. A new, more contagious variant of COVID-19 is spreading. If you get sick, the emergency room is full and the wait for a specialist is now months away.

- Crime and violence are on the rise. Police brutality is making national headlines. Murder, suicide, and substance abuse are all skyrocketing.

- In most towns, the restaurants are only open some days. The "great resignation" means there are not enough wait staff or cooks. Should we tip the person who takes my dinner order at the counter? Service seems to be a thing of the past.

- At the grocery and gas station double digit inflation is making a mess of household budgets. My daughter's annual tuition at Tulane is now above $80,000. Is college getting out of reach for all but the mega-rich?

Are we dreaming about proactive mental health? Is it possible to be sane in a world gone mad? Given the rapid rise in mental illness underway, it is clear we are heading in the wrong direction.

Can we create a safe harbor at work? *We Flourish* provides a roadmap and strategies for creating a proactive mental health culture.

- You can help your employees to pursue their proactive mental health goals. Your peer support skills could help them stay on track.

- You could create a better social climate at work. With a sense of community your people will trust one another, care for one another in times of need, and get to know one another. With a shared vision your people will feel inspired by their work, recognize workplace values, and feel that their personal values are consistent with what they do. With a positive outlook your people will cheer one another on, address challenges with enthusiasm and have some fun.

- You could align team policies and practices with proactive mental health. All 14 cultural touchpoints represent opportunities to shift cultural norms and nudge your people towards happier, healthier, and more productive lives.

- You could co-create an annual culture change plan that will, over time, maintain a proactive mental health culture. You could grow a bumper crop of safety, adaptability, connection, health behavior, purpose, and presence norms. Like a successful farmer, you could prepare the soil, plant the seed, nurture that growing crop, and harvest the fruit of your labor. You will not be cultivating fruits and vegetables, but you will be creating good earth for your team to achieve proactive mental health.

The vision of creating a proactive mental health culture was born out of necessity. Our mental health problems are exploding. Our treatment options are limited. We can't afford a larger bill. In a tight labor market, we can't just push mental illness under the rug or, worse yet, fire those afflicted.

Where and when do we address mental health needs? At first glance, workplaces seem like an unlikely place to begin. Many people are reluctant to discuss their personal problems at work. Most managers are uncomfortable assisting their employees with their mental illness challenges. Helping people address personal problems has its limitations. This is especially true at work when we are busy making things and serving customers.

Creating a proactive mental health workplace culture is a great addition to your current efforts. We can build islands of sanity in an otherwise complicated world. We can co-create social environments that reduce the stressors likely to make people sick. In addition, a proactive mental health culture will enhance resilience and grit. And we can enhance our culture-building capacity. We can develop the skills and tools needed to handle future proactive mental health challenges.

End Notes

Chapter 1

Merriam-Webster, "Flourish." *Merriam-Webster.com Dictionary*. https://www.merriam-webster.com/dictionary/flourish. Accessed 24 May, 2022.

American Psychological Association, "Stress in America™ 2020," *APA.org. https://www.apa.org/news/press/releases/stress/2020/report-october*.

National Institute of Mental Health Statistics. https://www.nimh.nih.gov/health/statistics/mental-illness.

Mental Health First Aid from National Council for Mental Wellbeing. https://www.mentalhealthfirstaid.org/2019/02/5-surprising-mental-health-statistics/#:~:-text=In%20the%20United%20States%2C%20almost,equivalent%20to%2043.8%20million%20people.

The Lancet Commissions, Vol. 392, Issue 10157, 1553-1598, October 27, 2018.

"Mental Health for global prosperity: We cannot afford to ignore the impact of mental health on the global economy." *Policy Brief*. Mental Health Innovation Network, Centre for Global Mental Health, London, UK: London School of Hygiene & Tropical Medicine, 2019.

Maddy Reinert, Theresa Nguyen and Danielle Fritze. 2021 *The State of Mental Health in America*. Mental Health American, Inc. 2020.

National Institute for Mental Health on Caring for Your Mental Health (2022). https://www.nimh.nih.gov/ health/topics/caring-for-your-mental-health.

World Health Organization's Definition of Health. (2022). https://www.who.int/news-room/fact-sheets/detail/ mental-health-strengthening-our-response#:~:tex- t=The%20WHO%20constitution%20states%3A%20 %22Health,of%20mental%20disorders%20or%20 disabilities.

"Mental Health: Culture, Race, and Ethnicity: A Supplement to Mental Health." *A Report of the Surgeon General*. Office of the Surgeon General (US); Center for Mental Health Services (US); National Institute of Mental Health (US). Rockville (MD): Substance Abuse and Mental Health Services Administration (US); 2001 Aug.

Fabius R, Frazee S, Thayer D, Kirshenbaum D, Reynolds J. "The Correlation of a corporate culture of health assessment score and health care cost trends." *J Occupational Health Environ Med*. 2018; 60:507–514.

Flynn J, Gascon G, Doyle S, et al. "Supporting a culture of health in the workplace: a review of evidence-based elements." *Am J Health Promotion*. 2018; 32:1755–1788.

Terry, PE, Seaverson, EL, Gossmeier J, Anderson Dr. "Association between nine quality components and superior worksite health management results." *Journal of Occupational and Environmental Medicine.* 2008.

Henke R, Head M, Kent K, Goetzel R, Roemer E, McCleary K. "Improvements in an organization's culture of health reduces workers' health risk profile and health care utilization." *Journal of Occupational and Environmental Medicine.* 2019; 61:96–101.

Kent K, Goetzel R, Roemer E, et al. "Developing two cultures of health measurement tools. Examining employers' efforts to influence population health inside and outside company walls." *Journal of Occupational and Environmental Medicine.* 2018; 60:1087–1097.

TC Pellmar, Brandt EN, Baird MA. "Health and behavior: The interplay of biological, behavioral, and social influences: Summary of the Institute of Medicine report." *The American Journal of Health Promotion.* 2002; 16:206-219.

Chapter 2

Robert F. Allen, Harry N. Dubin, Saul Pilnick, and Adella C. Youtz (1970). *Collegefields: From Delinquency to Freedom.* Special Child Publications, Inc., Seattle Washington.

Sara Harris & Robert F. Allen (1978). *The Quiet Revolution: The Story of a Small Miracle in American Life.* Rawson Associates Publishers, Inc., New York.

Robert F. Allen with Charlotte Kraft (1980). *Beat the System! A Way to Create More Human Environments.* New York, McGraw-Hill Book Company.

Robert F. Allen with Shirley Linde (1981). *Lifegain: The Exciting New Program that Will Change Your Health and Your Life*. New York: Appleton-Century-Crofts.

Robert F. Allen, Charlotte Kraft, Judd Allen, and Barry Certner (1987). *The Organizational Unconscious: How to Create the Corporate Culture You Want and Need*. Burlington, Vermont, Human Resources Institute Press.

Judd Allen. Books, journal articles and movies available at www.healthyculture.com.

Robert Levering and Milton Moskowitz (1994). *The 100 Best Companies to Work for in America* 3rd Revised Edition, New York: Plume Books.

Studs Terkel (1972). *Working: People Talk About What They Do All Day and How They Feel About What They Do*, New York: Ballantine Books.

John Bowe, Marisa Bowe, Sabin Streeter with Daron Murphy, and Rose Kernochan. *Gig: Americans Talk About Their Jobs*, New York: Three Rivers Press, 2001.

Chapter 4

Homer. *The Odyssey*. London and New York: W. Heinemann; G.P. Putnam's Sons, 1919.

Chapter 5

Dean Ornish (1998). Love & Survival: *The Scientific Basis for the Healing Power of Intimacy*. New York: Harper Collins.

Don Cohen and Laurence Prusak (2001). *In Good Company: How Social Capital Makes Organizations Work*. Boston: Harvard Business School Press.

Moos, R. (1973). "Conceptualization of human environments." *American Psychologist*, New York: John Wiley & Sons.

Robert Allen and Judd Allen (1987). "A sense of community, a shared vision and a positive culture: Core enabling factors in successful culture-based health promotion." *American Journal of Health Promotion*. Vol. 1, No. 3, pp. 40-47.

Marcus Buckingham and Curtis Coffman (1999). *First, Break All the Rules: What the World's Greatest Managers Do Differently*. New York: Simon & Schuster.

Robert Putnam (2000). *Bowling Alone: The Collapse and Revival of American Community*. New York: Simon & Schuster.

Charles H. Vogl (2016). *The Art of Community: Seven Principles for Belonging*. Oakland, California: Barrett-Koehler Publishers, Inc.

Martin E. P. Seligman (1972). "Learned Helplessness." *Annual Review of Medicine*. 23:407-412.

Martin E.P. Seligman (2006). *Learned Optimism: How to change your mind and your life*. New York: Vintage Books.

Chapter 6

Émile Durkheim (1851). *Suicide*. New York: Free Press.

About the Author

JUDD ALLEN EARNED his Ph.D. in community psychology from New York University. He is president of the Human Resources Institute, HealthyCultureNow, LLC and an editor of the *American Journal of Health Promotion*. His previous books include *Wellness Leadership, Culture Change Planner, Bringing Wellness Home, Kitchen Table Talks for Wellness, 103 Challenges for Manager-Led Wellness*, and *Healthy Habits Helpful Friends*. He lives in Burlington, Vermont and Montreal, Canada.

Made in the USA
Middletown, DE
26 September 2022

11231028R00116